New Perspectives on Worship Today

by the same author

Christians, Politics and Violent Revolution
A Dictionary of Liturgy and Worship
(*Editor*)
Every Day God
The Secular Use of Church Buildings

J G DAVIES

New Perspectives on Worship Today

SCM PRESS LTD

334 011310

First published 1978
by SCM Press Ltd
58 Bloomsbury Street, London WC1

Printed in Great Britain by
Richard Clay (the Chaucer Press) Ltd,
Bungay, Suffolk

CONTENTS

PREFACE

Is it possible in this day and age to say anything new about worship? To judge from the immense number of books devoted to the subject, many of which cover identical ground and say more or less the same thing, the chances of discovering any fresh perspectives are not very high. Nevertheless it is perhaps worth raising the further question or questions: how can anyone set about engaging in *creative* thinking about worship, or indeed, in creative thinking about any subject? Is there a method to be used that gives some promise of providing, not a rehash of the same old ideas, but some glimpses of fresh illumination? As a matter of fact there are at least two ways that would seem to be worth trying.

The first method of creative thinking, which has been worked out especially in the United States over the past fifteen years,[1] requires *divergent* thinking. What this means is that you bring together subjects that are not usually related. You concentrate your attention upon apparently disparate topics. The resulting thought process is then not convergent, i.e. it is not concerned with looking at two things together which in any case are normally linked; rather the process is divergent, i.e. it examines one item in conjunction with another with which it is seldom if ever associated. To illustrate this let me point to so-called liberation theology. What has happened is that the subject of salvation, which had been spiritualized and moralized and was usually conceived to refer to a future life or to the inner private life of the individual, has been related to the public world of contemporary politics, although this, in its turn, had been regarded as outside the sphere of direct religious concern. Who can doubt that the association of two such apparently divergent topics has resulted in creative thinking both in terms of the Latin American situation and a Black Theology?

The second method of creative thinking, which is somewhat

similar to this divergent approach, has been elaborated by Arthur
Koestler in *The Act of Creation*.[2] This requires the transference of
a particular subject from its usual frame of reference in order to
look at it in a new and unfamiliar matrix. When this is done, the
possibility is opened up of perceiving aspects that had previously
passed unnoticed, but now, because it is being regarded from a
new perspective, fresh insights may be obtained. A very telling
example of this is provided by the story of the discovery of the
difference between tartaric and paratartaric acids. Working within
the accepted theoretical framework, the celebrated German crystal-
lographer, Eilhardt Mitscherlich, affirmed that the salts are identical in all particulars, except that they behave differently towards
polarized light. The two, he affirmed, have the same chemical
composition and the same crystalline shape. Louis Pasteur however examined the salts within another matrix of thought. He
started from the view that different optical activity must be associated with irregularities in shape, and it was from this perspective
that he undertook a fresh systematic observation of tartaric and
paratartaric acid crystals. He immediately detected small facets on
them similar to those on quartz – these had entirely escaped the
notice of Mitscherlich. Transfer the subject to an unfamiliar frame
of reference and creativity becomes possible.

In this book I have used both these methods in tackling the subject of worship. In other words I have both considered it in conjunction with other topics with which it is not usually linked and
also I have on occasion removed it from its normal ecclesiastical
and traditional frame to examine it in fresh ones. This change-of-
matrix method is primary in the first chapter which interprets
worship in terms of games theory. In the last but one chapter it is
reviewed as a political act, after being analysed in the previous one
in the light of conflict theory. Here then worship is being looked
at in unfamiliar frames of reference. In other chapters the divergent method is to the fore with worship being considered in relation to what many may regard as disparate subjects; dance and
worship – does not dance detract from the supposed solemn ethos
of worship? Sexuality and worship – does not one have to leave
one's gender at the church door or suppose that we are all males
(and not homosexuals at that)? Laughter and worship – what,
smiles in the sanctuary!

Whichever method is actually used, the pattern of each chapter is the same. First of all the new matrix or the divergent topic is explored and defined and then these findings are related to worship. So, for example, the nature of play is examined before interpreting worship in terms of games theory, while the attempt is made to set out the meaning of dance before raising the question of its relationship to the cultus. There are similar initial analyses of sexuality, conflict, politics and humour, for it is only *after* working through to an understanding of these that it becomes possible to relate them to worship or worship to them.

Of course one of the difficulties of this methodology is to know where to start. What divergent topics should one select? There is of course no one 'correct' answer to this, and all that I can do is explain how I began and how one chapter connects with another. The idea that worship is in some sense a form of play is not new. In the present century, for example, it was suggested as long ago as 1918 by that great pillar of the Liturgical Movement Romano Guardini. But while several other writers have taken up his insight, it has not been developed in any real depth. Here then seemed a profitable point of departure – play and worship. Once I had started with this, the rest followed more or less as parts of a logical sequence.

Play, as I shall argue, is characterized by a balance between freedom and rules: between discharge and order. To analyse worship in these terms is to perceive that, like play, it too must embrace the whole being. One activity that achieves precisely this – that does involve each one of us as a psychosomatic entity – is dancing: so play leads to dance, itself a form of play, and then to sexuality, since dance has an inescapable erotic quality. In the course of this discussion I shall be looking at the possible sexual connotation of the kiss of peace which itself prompts the paying of attention to harmony and so to its apparent opposite, viz. conflict. It is this last subject therefore that naturally presents itself for the ensuing analysis, with particular concentration upon its positive effects in order to link these with our understanding of worship. But conflict may relate, from one aspect, to political struggle to change those features in public life that deny the demands of the Kingdom which is itself anticipated in the eucharist. So the next link in the logical chain is to look at the eucharist as a political act. The final chapter stands a little apart in that it does not necessarily follow from a consideration of politics, but the subject of laughter is in fact relevant to most of what I have written. Humour can be creative in itself, springing, like creativity, from the bisociation of two different matrices; play is almost unthinkable without some smiles and so is dance. Further to allow for conflict and political discussion without the safety valve of laughter is to court the danger of lack of proportion.

In the epilogue I have drawn attention to some recurring topics that, in addition to the logical sequence, serve to unite the several sections viz. the celebrative character of the eucharist, creativity, and the ideas of newness, change, identity, salvation, freedom, risk and participation. Two of these – participation and creativity – I have selected as in need of further elaboration.

Finally I must here acknowledge that neither of the two methods I have used guarantees that new perspectives will emerge. How far this procedure has enabled me to produce creative ideas must be left to the reader to judge – but at least this approach opens the door to the possibility. If I have failed, I hope I may nevertheless communicate some of the enjoyment I have derived from pursuing my studies along these lines.

J. G. DAVIES

University of Birmingham

I

Play and Worship

Although my intention in this book is to present some new perspectives on worship, it has to be admitted that understanding it as a game is not novel. As long ago as 1918 Romano Guardini published *The Spirit of the Liturgy*[1] and this contained a section entitled 'The Playfulness of the Liturgy'. In 1944 there appeared J. Huizinga's *Homo Ludens. A Study of the Play-Element in Culture*[2] and in this ritual is described as a game. Five years later, Hugo Rahner – in *Man at Play* – spoke of the liturgy as 'the playing of the Church',[3] while even more recently Robert E. Neale has followed Huizinga in interpreting ritual in the light of games theory.[4] However, as far as I am aware, no one has hitherto applied these generalizations in detail to Christian worship. It is one thing to assert that worship is a game; it is another to spell out what this means for our understanding of this central activity of the church.

Of course to some such an enterprise is a questionable undertaking. In part such a doubt may arise from a lack of knowledge of the extent to which games theory has been and is being taken seriously in a whole range of disciplines. For example, it is being used in connection with psychology, sociology, economics, literary criticism and even mathematics.[5] However many Christians may point to the word liturgy itself and argue that its derivation places the concept within the sphere of work rather than of play. It is indeed true that liturgy comes from the Greek words *leitos* meaning of or for the people and *ergon* meaning work. Liturgy is therefore basically a public service. It was given a cultic association in the Septuagint – the Greek translation of the Old Testament – where the liturgy of the Levites is to organize the temple worship on behalf of the people of God (e.g. I Chron. 6.48). Yet in the New Testament it is never applied to Christian worship as such but to the service of human beings (e.g. Phil. 2.30). Indeed it was not until the end of the second century that it entered theological vocabulary and was referred to worship in general, and only in the fourth century was it used specifically of the eucharist. In the light of this it seems to me quite plain that the derivation of the word liturgy is not sufficient in itself to preclude a consideration of worship in terms of play.

Nevertheless some will recall Paul's dictum: 'When I was a child, I spoke like a child, I thought like a child, I reasoned like a child; when I became a man, I gave up childish ways' (I Cor. 13.11). Play, to such people, is part and parcel of these childish ways which are to be given up as one matures. Play is a diversion, a distraction, and is less significant than other activities. To play when others are at work is a sign of uninvolvement and irresponsibility. The adult who behaves like this is scornfully dismissed as a playboy. Such a view, however, is one engendered in a society dominated by a work ideology or, more specifically, by the Protestant ethic which falsely regarded leisure as sinful and work alone as to the glory of God.[6] This attitude fails to take account of the seriousness of play – watch a chess player making a move and his earnestness is immediately apparent. The one who plays, to use a portmanteau Greek word in translation, is a 'grave-merry' person, i.e. one in whom seriousness and gaiety are mixed. Light-heartedness is present – as indicated by the word 'playful' – but the complete absorption in the activity by the true player is anything but superficial. Indeed it is reasonable to hold that play is of a higher order than seriousness, because seriousness attempts to exclude play whereas play as I have just indicated, can include seriousness.

Of course in our Western society a work ideology is completely transforming many spheres of play so that they are ceasing to be what they were. The spirit of play is more akin to amateurism than to that professionalism which is progressively superseding it and sees games exclusively as so many different forms of work. The lightheartedness of a game of football or cricket is tending to become a thing of the past. But then, as Roger Caillois has pointed out, 'games illustrate the moral and intellectual values of a culture. Further they contribute to their more precise definition and to their development'.[7] So in Western capitalist culture where the profit motive is the supreme value and hard work to increase the Gross National Product is the ideal, it is to be expected that games will embody a similar outlook with large transfer fees hitting the headlines and games becoming the 'work' of those who engage in them for their livelihood.

The integrity and maturity of the one who fully manifests not the spirit of professionalism but the spirit of play are not easy to achieve. According to Rahner they can only be acquired by one 'who neither cynically despises the world nor is consumed by an epicurean appetite for it; he must be a man who has the divine so much at the centre of his preoccupation that he can find it in the things of this world'.[8] This has nothing to do with childishness. Yet whether or not worship may be rightly understood from the point of view of games theory is a matter for demonstration. The final answer to those who would dismiss play as childish can only be provided by an analysis of the concept and by seeking to apply it to the cultus. We turn then immediately to the modern understanding of play and to a definition of its characteristics.

According to Huizinga, play is (*i*) a voluntary activity which is (*ii*) an exercise of freedom, even when (*iii*) conducted according to certain rules. It is (*iv*) disinterested, in the sense that it is satisfying in itself and so adorns life. (*v*) While based upon the ordinary it is obviously somewhat extra-ordinary and has limits of space. (*vi*) It demands the use of the imagination and expresses the participants' interpretation of life and the world, thus creating its own community, i.e. it promotes the formation of social groupings. Finally, (*vii*) it has a 'fun element' that defies precise analysis but, as we have seen, does not exclude seriousness.[9]

In the steps of Huizinga, Caillois has schematized the formal characteristics of play under six headings. These are virtually the same as the first six of Huizinga's list and so I reproduce them here following Huizinga's order and using the same enumeration:

(*i*) It is free. No one is obliged to play.

(*ii*) It is uncertain. The outcome cannot be known in advance, for the precise sequence of actions is not predetermined.

(*iii*) It is subject to its own rules.

(*iv*) It is unproductive. It does not create goods or wealth.

(*v*) It is separate. It is circumscribed by a fixed place and time.

(*vi*) It is fictitious. This means that it does not merely repeat normal routine although it may copy and be based upon daily life.[10]

Now these are in fact characteristics not only of play but of liturgy. Thus (*i*) worship is an activity freely undertaken, but its outcome (*ii*) is by no means known in advance for, as Robert Neale expresses it, 'sacramental ritual is never effective automatically as the magician would like to believe, but depends upon the spirit of both man and the gods to make it a holy adventure. This fact is acknowledged by the player.'[11] Worship (*iii*) certainly has its own rules, and hence Guardini affirms that 'the liturgy has laid down the serious rules of the sacred game which the soul plays before God'.[12] But such worship (*iv*) is not creative of goods or wealth. It does occur (*v*) in a fixed space – e.g. a church building – and at a predetermined time. It has too (*vi*) a certain fictitious or imitatory element, in that the eucharist is based upon a meal but is not an exact reproduction of one.

This brief summary should be sufficient to indicate what is meant by the general thesis that worship is a game. But we must go further. We have to move from the characteristics to the meaning of play and then seek to apply this to liturgy. Many writers on play approach it from a purely utilitarian point of view. So they understand it as refreshment, as that which produces pleasure, rest and restoration. But to define the meaning of play in this manner is simply to regard it as another form of work, for play is then not being considered for its own sake; it is simply useful as contributing to some activity outside itself. It is, for example, a form of recreation that makes us fitter to return to work. Worship, of course, can be and often is interpreted in this way. So it is regarded as an occasion for the gathering of the Christian community that its members may, as it were, recharge their spiritual batteries and so be better able to continue their witness in the world outside. Worship then is related to mission in terms of gathering and sending. But just as to regard play as incidental to work is not to examine play in itself, so to formulate the meaning of worship in this way is not to understand it in itself. If worship is a game, and we are to do justice to this concept, the idea of gathering and sending simply will not do. Indeed, since the understanding of worship as a game serves to demonstrate the falsity of this interpretation, it has already proved its value. But it is possible to go much further than this.

How are we to understand play *in itself*? Here the investigations of Robert E. Neale, in the book referred to in the opening paragraph of this chapter, are of the utmost interest and relevance.

According to him, 'to speak of play is to speak of the nature of man'.[13] This nature, he contends, has two poles: the one consists of the need to discharge energy and the other of the need to organize or design experience. These two frequently conflict and if either one or the other dominates then equilibrium is not achieved. So when the need to discharge is to the fore, the individual can be overwhelmed by the accidental and knows only random events; whereas if the need for design is prior, the individual is enslaved by generalizations and becomes so rigidly attached to the formal that discharge is inhibited and the inner life is lethargic. Yet this conflict is not inevitable: according to Neale in play each may be assigned its limits and may assist rather than perturb the other:

> In this situation, the need for discharge is met and the need for design is empowered; at the same time the need for design is met and the need for discharge organized. . . . Harmony occurs when the needs for discharge and design both accept their limits and excite each other. Under these conditions, the individual experiences a fuller power and order. There is neither wildness nor lethargy, chaos nor rigidity, but a coalescence of discharge and design that creates meaningful and graceful movement. Such activity is play.[14]

Neale thus understands play *in itself* as an activity that harmonizes the discharge of energy with the experience of design. So he brings to the fore two of the formal characteristics specified by Caillois – items (*i*) and (*iii*) – namely, freedom and the observance of rules. Clearly this balanced interplay of the two poles requires the rejection both of a random discharge of energy, which does not make for meaningful activity, and a rigid design of experience, that does not allow spontaneity and freshness. Impulsive chaos at one extreme contrasts with compulsive routine at the other, while in play discharge is organized and design is energized.

A very similar interpretation of play was propounded as long ago as 1795 by Friedrich Schiller. In his *Letters on the Aesthetic Education of Man*, Schiller set out from the distinction between what he called the sensuous drive and the formal drive. These correspond exactly with Neale's discharge and design. Schiller further contended that the two may be harmonized by means of the play drive,[15] just as Neale points to play as the means of achieving an equilibrium between the two poles. Hence Schiller's conclusion was that 'man only plays when he is in the fullest sense of the word a human being, and he is only fully a human being when he plays'.[16]

If an initial application of this to worship is now attempted, it will readily be seen that worship itself can be understood and practised in terms of these two poles or drives in isolation – in which case it is unbalanced – or in terms of their harmony – in which case by definition worship is a game. If worship is regarded as no more than a happening, it becomes a random discharge of energy without any rules whatsoever. If worship is conducted exclusively in accordance with a fixed liturgy, i.e. with rules dictating everything, it must lack freshness and newness. The first extreme evacuates worship of meaning, while the second organizes it in a plodding and rigid manner which denies creativity – indeed does not even allow for it – and also denies recreation. Worship as a happening becomes impulsive chaos, while if the element of freedom is entirely restricted by fixed forms it becomes compulsive routine.

All this means that for worship to be truly itself as a game, it must have certain basic rules, but their function is to provide a minimal structure within which there may be considerable latitude for response, i.e. the rules of liturgy are to constitute a framework (design) for freedom (discharge of energy).

It is a fact worthy of note that the apostle Paul seems to have understood worship precisely in this way, although naturally he did not employ this particular terminology. The evidence for this is writ large in his first epistle to the Corinthians. It is apparent from this that the services of the Corinthian congregation involved an immense discharge of energy which was in danger of producing chaos. Paul set himself the task of providing certain minimal rules that would avoid this, while still allowing a large measure of freedom. In other words, he sought to balance discharge or sensuousness with design or formality.

As regards discharge, Paul was concerned with the speaking in tongues and prophesying, and these apparently presented a twofold problem: first, many were speaking at the same time so that no one was being edified and, second, many were engaging in glossolalia without an interpreter and so the utterances were unintelligible. So he asks: 'If the whole church assembles and all speak in tongues, and outsiders or unbelievers enter, will they not say that you are mad?' (I Cor. 14.23). Indeed if everyone is giving tongue the effect will be like bugles venting indistinct sounds; indeed 'you will be speaking into the air' (14.8f.). In similar vein if a number prophesy at the same time, few will derive any benefit from the resulting confusion or babble. Further lack of harmony was being displayed by the rich not sharing their food with the poor at the eucharist, with an excessive individualism so that 'each one goes ahead with his own meal, and one is hungry and another is drunk' (11.21).

To cope with this situation of random discharge – which is one extreme pole of human nature – Paul laid down certain rules. These rules themselves stemmed from certain principles which he also enunciated briefly. They may be formulated in this way:

Principle I The language of worship must be understandable; indeed what is said must be capable of being comprehended even by an outsider (14.16).

Principle II 'All things be done for edification' (14.26) – this is obviously closely allied to the first principle.

Principle III 'All things should be done decently and in order' (14.40) because 'God is not a God of confusion but of peace' (14.33).

Principle IV Worship is to be a manifestation and deepening of Christian fellowship and unity – there are to be 'no divisions among you' (cf. 11.20), since 'because there is one loaf, we who are many are one body, for we all partake of the one loaf' (10.17).

Principle V Every worshipper should make his own contribution. 'When you come together, each one has a hymn, a lesson, a revelation, a tongue, or an interpretation', (14.26) i.e. worship is an activity in which all have parts to play.

These principles are not of course set out in any systematic form; they are scattered throughout the various chapters and are closely connected with the particular rules of the liturgical game that Paul formulates. This close relationship of principle and rule will be readily appreciated. For example, it is a principle of football that it should be played without any deliberate physical harm; this is then embodied in the rules about fouls that seek to ensure this. Similarly the liturgical principle that 'all things be done for edification' finds expression in the first of Paul's rules, which may be listed as follows:

Rule I Speaking with tongues must be restricted, either by allowing only two or three to practise it if an interpreter be present or by not permitting anyone to engage in it if there is no interpreter at hand (14.27f.). This rule is a practical embodiment of Principles I and II.

Rule II If any are moved to prophesy, the persons concerned must do this in turns – and in any case no more than two or three on any one occasion. Moreover 'if a revelation is made to another sitting by, let the first be silent' (14.29f.). This expresses Principle III.

Rule III The eucharist is to follow the pattern of the Last Supper (11.23–26).

Rule IV Consequently the eating and drinking must take place by all at the same time and there must be a fair share of food (11.21). This embodies Principle IV.

To these four rules Paul added three others, which are to be noted for the sake of completeness although they do not derive from his basic principles but are conditioned by the cultural outlook of his day.

Rule V Women should have their heads covered at services (11.6).

Rule VI Men should not wear hats (11.7).

Rule VII Women should keep silent (14.34).

While seeking to ensure design in this way, Paul was also concerned not to exclude freedom. Speaking with tongues and prophecy are permitted under the conditions laid down (Rules I and II). Moreover everyone is at liberty to make a contribution (Principle V). In this way Paul sought to balance discharge and order. He endorsed the freedom of individual participation but devised minimal rules to prevent this degenerating into a random furore. So discharge was organized and the possibility was open for design to be energized. The rules guaranteed significant identity and meaningful movement without reducing the worshippers to a completely passive observance of some fixed form.

The history of the development of the liturgy is in part an account of how some of these Pauline principles and rules were progressively ignored. When the eucharist was transferred from

the house-church to the basilica, it ceased to be a domestic affair
celebrated by a group in primary relations and became a public
event observed by a vast congregation, many of whom, in the
nature of things, could not know one another. What is suitable
within the relatively intimate atmosphere of a living room becomes
unfitting within the spacious surroundings of a large monumental
hall. In the pre-Constantinian era there was a generally observed
structure of worship (rules) and there was still considerable freedom (discharge); even Hippolytus indicated that he was providing
only a model and not an unvariable text.[17] But in the latter half of
the fourth century fixed orders began to emerge. Stylization suitable to the new architectural setting was necessary when the
eucharist became observed by hundreds of spectators rather than
being performed by participants.[18] The pole of design thus pre-
dominated and that of discharge was neglected.[19]* Worship then
ceased to be a game played by the worshippers. In so far as it
remained a game in any sense at all it was one played by a small
group of professionals in front of a passive audience.

Something must now be said briefly about the bearing of this on
the subject of worship today – many centuries after Paul wrote his
directions for Corinth. Rules, says Caillois, 'are inseparable from a
game as soon as it acquires an institutional existence. From that
moment the rules are part of the very nature of the game . . . Nevertheless at the origin of a game is a primary freedom.'[20] However
what we have witnessed over the centuries in the main line churches
has been a takeover of the game of worship by the rules themselves.
Fixed liturgies, where absolutely everything is prescribed, have
excluded the possibility of freshness and response. While any game
including that of worship, has to have rules which must be accepted,
they should be as unobtrusive as possible and should allow free
action within them. The rules of golf, for example, do not reduce
the players to puppets. If, to recall some of the formal characteristics of play, it is by its very nature a free and voluntary activity,
if it is to be a source of joy and if it has a certain spontaneity, one
must question the continued production of revised liturgies[21] which
do no more than perpetuate the regimentation of congregations
with no possibility of discharge of energy. Then worship ceases
to be the game it should be and becomes a form of work. Indeed
it is perhaps relevant to note that the Benedictines referred to the
Divine Office as *opus Dei* – the work of God: some might say it was

hard labour! What is required is neither the unbridled license of
some worship happenings in the underground church nor the
straightjacket of entirely predetermined forms in the main-line
churches which inevitably lead to what Max Weber has called
'spectator religion' that has little influence upon those present
because it provides no inner motivation.[22]

If games theory helps in this way towards the adoption of a
vantage point from which to criticize – in, I hope, a constructive
manner – much that goes by the name of worship at the present
day, it has other relevant aspects to be taken into account. Return-
ing to Neale's valuable exposition, we find him maintaining that
to play is to engage in an adventure. If this be applied to worship
what fresh insights then emerge?

Play, according to Neale, is an adventure because it is challeng-
ing and its outcome is uncertain. As adventure, play allows for
spontaneity, surprise and novelty and all these are out of place in
the world of work and appear threatening to normality. Within
play understood as adventure there are four closely related elements. These elements are the product of the harmony of the needs
for discharge of energy and design of experience. They are peace,
freedom, delight and illusion,[23] and to each of these in turn I shall
now give some brief consideration.

Peace is the outcome of the unification of the basic needs. Such
peace is not passivity but a condition of meaningful activity. 'The
peace of play is peaceful action. The perversion of this attitude is
the "peace" of *in*action. . . . Rigid control by the need for design
may appear as peaceful. In this case it is not the peace of harmony,
but only an apparent calm.'[24] Such peace is interpersonal and so is
to be attained in union with one's fellow players. Nor does it
exclude the recognition of conflict nor prevent engagement in it,
but it does enable the players not to feel threatened by it and to
become involved in it with confidence in the outcome. This peace
within adventure/play corresponds exactly to the liturgical *pax*,
i.e. to that greeting which manifests and helps to bring about the
fellowship of the worshippers. This peace is the Hebrew *shalom*
which is a social happening, an event in interpersonal relations; but
it does not rule out, as I shall argue in a later chapter, contained
conflict.[25]

The freedom that Neale designates as the second element derives
from the liberation from the opposing drives of the two basic needs.

If either is in the ascendent, freedom is perverted. The 'impulsive individual feels free from control, and the rigid person feels free from chaos. . . . This freedom is freedom without hope. Further, there is an awareness that this freedom is really bondage, and one really becomes a slave of the dominant need.'[26] This is certainly the experience of many worshippers who have engaged regularly over a period of time in either random happenings or in entirely fixed orders of service. It is however particularly the latter that tend to be the most attractive both to primitives and to twentieth-century folk who find it difficult to adapt to change. According to Cazeneuve, 'the primitive seeks to enclose himself in a system of rules which can define for him a human condition free from anxiety'.[27] Worship then operates as a sedative and preserves a certain degree of social equilibrium; it functions in precisely the same way for those who seek a haven of security at the present day. But worship as a game is then denied its true character and becomes the celebration of unfreedom, whereas it should be an occasion when freedom to be oneself is enjoyed.

Precisely because there is this possibility of freedom in true play and true worship, there is a challenge, as in any adventure. The outcome is not foreclosed: the results are not predictable. There is a challenge in worship to use one's talents and so to exercise one's freedom, to build up community and to encounter God. The real worshipper, as he plays, is not then the unfortunate person of whom the limerick speaks.

> There was a young man who said, 'Damn!
> It appears to me now that I am
>   Just a being that moves
>   In predestinate grooves,
> Not a taxi, or bus, but a tram.'

To get off the lines is to take a risk, but when certain basic rules are accepted and adhered to the result need not be meaningless confusion.

The third element in play in terms of adventure is fun, joy, and even rapture. These are so many aspects of worship as a feast, with its predominant note of love and happiness. Two recent excellent studies of the festal character of worship obviate the need for further elaboration of this theme here, especially as I have in any case already written on the subject.[28] It is simply to be noted that when Frédéric Debuyst[29] and Harvey Cox[30] presented their exposition, they were in fact operating within the sphere of games theory.

Finally there is the element of illusion. This term is not to be understood in this context to refer to that which is false or make-believe, but in accordance with its strict etymology from *in* and *ludere*, i.e. to be in play. Illusion thus describes that situation of being apart from the world of work. This does not however imply other-worldliness but rather new-worldliness since it introduces people into a new dimension.[31] Hence worship is to be the realm of new discharge and new design; it is a playful response to the new world of possibility that is revealed in and through the game of cultus. In this respect worship is a game of liberation and as such it has to be devised imaginatively so that the worshippers are able to anticipate what can and shall be different and when in the process they break the bonds of the seemingly immutable *status quo*. As a game of liberation worship can afford us 'critical perspectives for change in an otherwise burdensome world'. It can 'open up creative freedom and future alternatives. We are then no longer playing merely with the past in order to escape it for a while, but we are increasingly playing with the future in order to get to know it.'[32]

It will perhaps be granted in the light of what has been said so far that worship is a game and that to understand it as such is to perceive some of its most essential aspects. However the question remains: what kind of game is it? Caillois has specified four main categories. First, there are games of competition, such as football. Second, there are games of chance, such as roulette. Third, there are games of imitation, such as charades. Fourth, there are games of vertigo, which he defines as rapid movement, like turning round on the spot and producing a state of confusion – such are the effects of swings or a roller-coaster.[33] These categories may be regarded as a continuum with two poles: at the one end highly disciplined, corresponding to the need for design, and at the other improvised and even anarchic, corresponding to the discharge of energy. In this respect Caillois' analysis comes close to that of Neale.

I must now attempt to use this typology of games to outline a corresponding typology of worship. This means that we have to consider what kinds of worship correspond with these different kinds of games. As regards the first category – games of competition – we may note that one form of ritual, practised for example by the Mormons and Jehovah's Witnesses, is that of witnessing and this in effect posits a state of competition in that every act of witness is a proclamation of faith against the non-believer.[34] Worship as witness then assumes the style of a competitive game either against the outsider or possibly, worse if anything, against one's fellow believers in an attempt to go one better than they. Competition can also imply conflict, but I will leave until a later chapter an examination of worship in the light of conflict theory and simply note here that a competitive game and a worship embodying conflict may be understood as a struggle conducted according to prescribed rules.

As regards games of chance, I do not propose to consider this in terms of Pascal's wager, i.e. that it is prudent to wager one's life on the existence of God since if he exists one wins and if he does not exist one has lost nothing that one would not have lost in any case. Rather the chance aspect of this type points to an essential aspect of all games, i.e. the outcome is uncertain. This equally applies to every act of worship. God is simply not at our disposal. He is free but so, in worship, must we be free and not forced into a rigid mould of liturgical conformity.

Leaving the third type aside for a moment, we may observe that the fourth kind – games of vertigo – finds its worshipping parallel in the Whirling Dervishes but it also has affinities with the devotional practices of certain Pentecostal groups with their rhythmic movements and their tendency to pass into a trance. It is however to the third type that the Christian eucharist most nearly corresponds, i.e. it is a game of imitation. This is to be understood in reference both to the concept that playtime is storytime and to the Christian tradition that sees the origin of the eucharist in the Last Supper.

Play, according to Neale, is a story lived by the player.[35] 'The verbal telling of a tale is only a sign of that more complete telling which engages the whole interest of the individual. Ultimately the story is told by a way of life.'[36] A story, too, is news; it discloses something novel or strange. Even when it is a story retold it can often have a freshness about it that is new. An adventure also is 'the living of the news, and it is this participation that is the full telling of the tale'.[37] The application of this to the eucharist is all

but self evident. The eucharist as playtime is also storytime. It is
the story of God in Christ and this story is good news – gospel –
which engages persons and becomes part of their life style. Moreover the story of Jesus is continuous – a serial if you like – it is not a
once-upon-a-time story that has been ended. The complete tale
of Jesus to date is not confined to the pages of the New Testament;
it includes what is still going on in and through human beings at all
times and in all places. It is too a story that speaks of the future for
the God of Jesus Christ is the God of the future who calls us towards
the fullness of his Kingdom. Christian worshippers live out this story
partly through imitation. It is as if a group of believers were to say
to one another: 'Let us play at the Last Supper.' The president
takes the part of Jesus and actually reproduces his actions in the
upper room by blessing God over the bread and wine, breaking the
former for distribution and handing round the elements. The
members of the congregation are the modern counterparts of the
apostles as they gather round the table. It was an appreciation of
this that induced many medieval theologians to interpret the mass
as a drama.[38] By playing the story of the Last Supper participants
acquire a significant identity as followers of Jesus and are strength-
ened in their discipleship for the story spills over into a way of life.

To recognize the imitative element in the eucharist is not to endorse the view that it is no more than an actualization in appearance
only, a sham reality. Rather it is an actualization by re-presentation,
to use Huizinga's phrase.[39] It enables the worshippers to be united
with Christ in his self-offering for the world: This is my body. . . .
This is my blood. The eucharist then is a re-presentation of the
Christ event in the sense of an *anamnesis* or re-calling, whereby
that event is made present here and now through its effects. The
eucharist is not just imitatory; it causes the worshippers to participate in the event itself, as they engage in this sacred game, and to
anticipate the longed-for future. This game, as I have already suggested, must have certain rules, which are to provide a minimal
framework or structure within which there should be considerable
latitude. We have seen some of the simple rules that Paul propounded and these provided for the need for design and at the
same time allowed discharge of energy. The structure of the
eucharist today could function in this way, allowing freedom within an overall pattern that itself prevents degeneration into chaos.

Before leaving this subject it should be noted, to quote Neale again, that 'the maturation of the individual presents the opportunity of going from playlessness to full play and that full play in the adult is religion'.[40] Full play he defines as that which 'uses all the potentialities at the particular development stage of the individual's physical, psychological and social growth'.[41] Hence full play relates to the creative exercise of one's gifts and the extent to which it engages the whole personality in interaction with other human beings. If the mind only is engaged, we have only partial play. This is what happens when worship is concerned solely with verbalization. In part this is the reason why so many people in the Western world find the worship on offer less and less satisfying and why the Pentecostalists, with their greater freedom of worshipping response and their use of contemporary cultural forms, attract a great number of people. Full worship, like full play, must engage the body and the emotions, as well as involving cerebral activity. There are numerous ways in which this may be achieved. One very obvious method is to adopt dancing into worship – but this is a subject in itself and it is to this we turn in the next chapter.

2
Dance and Worship

In seeking to associate the two subjects of worship and dance I am immediately faced with a question: where shall I begin? One possible and it might seem obvious starting point would be to continue the theme of the previous chapter and to accept with Huizinga that dance is 'the purest and most perfect form of play that exists . . . It is an integral part of play; the relationship is one of direct participation, almost of essential identity. Dancing is a particular and a particularly perfect form of playing.'[1] Conversely, Hugo Rahner asserts that 'all play has somewhere deep within it an element of the dance; it is a kind of dance round the truth. Sacred play has always taken the form of a dance, for in rhythm of body and music are conjoined all the possibilities of embodying and expressing in visible form the strivings and aspirations of the soul.'[2] Much that Huizinga says in his pioneer study of play can very easily be applied to dance, e.g. in 'play [dance] the beauty of the human body in motion reaches its zenith. In its more developed forms it is saturated with rhythm and harmony, the noblest gifts of aesthetic perception known to man.'[3]

Furthermore the characteristics of play, as defined by Huizinga and already listed in the previous chapter, are characteristics of dance. So it is a voluntary activity which is an exercise of freedom even when conducted according to certain rules. It is disinterested in the sense that it is satisfying in itself and so adorns life. While based upon the ordinary, it is itself somewhat extraordinary. It has limits of time and space. It creates its own community, i.e. it promotes the formation of social groupings. It demands the use of the imagination. It expresses the participants' interpretation of life and the world. Finally, it has a 'fun element' that 'defies analysis but does not exclude seriousness'.[4]

We find ourselves confronted at this juncture by a nexus of con-

cepts, viz. play, dance, ritual and feast. Thus Rust, from a utilitarian standpoint, declares that dance is a form of ritual,[5] while
Huizinga affirms that ritual is 'formally indistinguishable from
play'[6] and that the intimate relationship of play and feast is to be
seen in the action of dancing. 'All true ritual is sung, danced and
played.'[7] Already we are moving towards a legitimization of dance
as a proper and fitting component of Christian worship. However
despite Huizinga and even granting that dance may be a special
form of play, there is something about it that distinguishes it from
other games. Whatever the common characteristics, dance, after
all, is not the same as football nor as whist or bridge. Nor does it
fall neatly into the typology of games formulated by Caillois and
also listed in the previous chapter. It is scarcely a game of competition nor of chance; it has some aspects of imitation but that
does not exhaust its vocabulary; some dances may result in vertigo
but that is insufficient to provide a basis of meaning for all dance.

If then we do not accept games theory as our primary point of
reference, we are still left with the initial problem of where to
begin. Yet perhaps after all this is not so difficult to solve as it may
seem. I am a theologian and therefore presumably if I exercise my
profession I shall set out to propound a theology of the dance. But
such a statement could well give rise to three further questions. Is
it not rather highfalutin' to seek to formulate a theology of the
dance? In any case, what exactly is a theology of the dance? Indeed, is it not true – à la Gertrude Stein – that a dance is a dance
is a dance? Let us examine these three questions in turn and so
begin to open up further the subject of this chapter.

In the first place then: although theology covers a whole host of
specialized studies, each and every practitioner would wish to say
with Terence: *Homo sum: humani nihil a me alienum puto.* Believing
that humankind is the creation of God and that therefore the
reality of human beings is to be comprehended within the reality
of the divine, there is no aspect of everyday living which, in the
last analysis, can be said to fall outside the theologian's concern.
For a theologian to seek to propound a theology of the dance is no
more than to exercise his *métier* in relation to one particular human
activity. Whether the result is highfalutin' or not must be left to
the reader to decide.

In the second place: a theology of the dance is a formulation of
an understanding of it in the light of one's knowledge of God. It is,

then, an analysis of dance as a human activity and it is also an illumination of the meaning of that activity by relating it to God – to God, in Christian terms, both as Creator and Liberator. Simply to analyse dance as a human activity is not a theological enterprise, although it is basic to the theological enterprise. Simply to make some generalizations, relating this activity in a vague way to the divine, would be neither to illuminate its meaning nor to produce sound theological reflection. Instead, we have to be concerned with such questions as: what is dancing? what connection is there, if any, between it and God? What has God to do with dancing? To sum up: a theology of the dance is an attempt to explicate its meaning as a human activity in the light of the revelation of God in Christ. Further, in a chapter devoted to worship and dance, a theology of the latter must also seek to understand its place in the celebration of the liturgy. After all, worship is a response to God, and that response can assume many forms. A theology of the dance must therefore include a demonstration of how it can be understood as an appropriate form of response.

The third question was: is not a dance a dance? The answer is that of course it is, in the sense that it is a human activity the meaning of which is essentially to be sought *in itself*. In making such an admission I am immediately rejecting, in the steps of Paul Valéry,[8] a purely utilitarian approach to the subject. Utilitarian interpretations all start from the assumption that dance must serve something which is not dance. Thus F. Rust can say that it is a motor reaction to stimuli whose function is to express feeling or to work off energy.[9] Such a definition, and others like it, does not really deal with dance as dance. Granted that dancing involves physical movement, nevertheless it is not movement which has some objective beyond itself. In this respect dancing differs from many physical activities which can only be interpreted in terms of their objectives. So I may walk across a room in order to pick up a book: the purpose of my action is not in the movement itself but in my arriving at a place where I can take up an object and once I have accomplished this the movement is completed. But dance is not like that; I may stop dancing because I am tired, not because I have attained some objective outside the dance itself.[10] Similarly dancing may involve a discharge of energy, but so do physical jerks which are certainly not dance. Nor is it just a response to stimuli; it is a creative act. Indeed the utilitarian approach fails to take account of the fact that dance is a significant function, i.e. there is some sense to it. In dance there is something that transcends the immediate needs (biological or otherwise) of life and imparts meaning to the action. All dancing means something. Since it has meaning, this implies that it has a non-materialistic quality which is of the nature of the thing itself. Hence while it should be recognized that dancing is part of the innate human biological make-up, it must be added that in dance a biological rhythm is transformed into a voluntary rhythm that expresses meaning. Indeed, in an age dominated by utilitarian thinking one needs the counterbalancing effect of an activity in which one engages for its own sake and not for some other end outside itself. Dancing calls in question the barren solemnity of a purely utilitarian view of life.

In this last respect dancing has an affinity with worship. At a time when functional thinking is very much to the fore, it is of course possible to interpret worship also in terms of its functions: how does it work? What is its purpose? What does it set out to achieve? There is no harm in asking such questions, but they do not exhaust the meaning of worship, any more than they do of dance. Moreover if pursued exclusively these same questions can obscure its meaning. Worship has certain functions, but there is an overplus. From one aspect, as we have seen, it is more like a game than anything else, and so Romano Guardini could say of it that it is a kind of holy play (like dance) in which the person with utter abandonment 'learns to waste time for the sake of God'.[11]

However if we reject a simplistic utilitarian understanding of dance and insist that it has first to be interpreted in itself, the theologian, and especially one who derives his perspective from the Bible, has to make clear what for him *in itself* includes, by distinguishing between the Greek and the Hebrew or biblical way of looking at things. The Greek did, from a limited aspect, consider a thing in itself; he analysed it, dissected it, defined it in terms of what it is. He was concerned with its empirical nature, with its objective reality. The Hebrew considered a thing as it was in relation to himself. He was not concerned just with things as they are but with what he could make of them. He associated them with their end which he defined by his existence before God and their place in the divine purpose. He sought 'beyond the natural things what they have to say, their meaning, the will which is expressed by

them'.[12] Thus the Hebrew sought to comprehend the daily and
common reality in a reality more profound that has its foundation
in the will of God. So while in developing a theology of the dance,
once must begin with what dance is as a human activity, the biblical
perspective also requires that activity to be understood within its
total context in terms of its meaning in relation to the divine will.
Only then will an appreciation of dance in itself be completed.

What then is the essential nature of dance as a human activity?
Although this is the basic question, it is not easy to formulate an
answer simply because of the nature of dance itself. This is indicated in this extract from Paul Valéry's dialogue *Dance and the
Soul*. Socrates, watching someone dancing, asks: 'What in reality
is dance?' Eryximachus replies: 'Isn't it what we are looking at?
What do you want clearer about dancing than dancing itself?'[13]
Anna Pavlova was making the same point when, asked what she
was saying in a particular dance, she retorted: 'If I could tell you, I
would not dance.'[14] In other words dance is not just one more
discursive language, expressing something that could equally well
be said in another language. Rather it is a non-discursive language
and in the final analysis can never be completely translated into
words and concepts. Discursive language, which is the kind we
think and talk in, passes from premises to conclusions and expresses rationality. Non-discursive language, which embraces most
of the arts including dance, refers to things that aie hard to talk
about and that cannot easily be put into matter-of-fact statements.
So Martha Graham could assert that 'dance is not a literary art and
is not given to words . . . it is something you do. There is danger in
rationalizing about it too much.'[15]

Dance then is not concerned with conveying information; on the
contrary it is itself a form of exploration. In dance we discover
what we as physical beings can and will do. 'Movement in the
modern dance' – so Martha Graham again – 'is the product not of
invention but of discovery . . . discovery of what the body will do,
and what it can do in the expression of emotions.'[16] She further
declared: 'You experience, you find out and it tells you what it
means. . . . You move in such a way that it gives you back anger or
grief.' In other words, dance is not just expression. A dancer does
not say: I want to express anger which I fully understand and now
I am doing so. Rather he or she comes to know more deeply what
anger is by dancing it. So just as there can be mental exploration,
there can be physical exploration in terms of dance.

However, granted that dance may be exploratory and is non-discursive, and granted that it is consequently difficult to define its exact nature in words, nevertheless I propose to make the attempt by drawing upon the reflections of those modern practitioners of the art who have themselves used words to convey something of its meaning.

Modern dance is the creation of an outstanding group of pioneers which includes Isadora Duncan, Ruth Saint-Denis, Martha Graham, Mary Wigman and Doris Humphrey. In a remarkable study – *Danser sa vie* – R. Garaudy summarizes their common understanding to the effect that dance is 'the expression, by organized movements of the body in meaningful sequences, of experiences which transcend the power of words and mime'.[17] According to Isadora Duncan, rebutting a German impresario anxious to exploit her talents, 'I had come to Europe to bring about a great renaissance of religion through the Dance, to bring the knowledge of the Beauty and Holiness of the human body through its expression of movements, and not to dance to the amusement of overfed bourgeoisie after dinner.'[18] Similarly Martha Graham, in a television interview when she was speaking about her ballet 'Adoration', asserted: 'I want to show the glory of the body in action and in stillness.' To her the dancer is 'a divine athlete'. According to François Delsarte, who devoted his life to classifying bodily movements and their meaning: 'To every manifestation of the body there corresponds an interior manifestation of the spirit.'[19] So, to quote Garaudy further, these pioneers understand dance as 'the realization of the unity of the interior life and the exterior life, integrated into a unique action'.[20] Thus while we in the West tend to distinguish between the internal or spiritual and the outward and physical, dance may be understood as a form of the interior life but one over which physiology is dominant, i.e. through dance the interior life is embodied in the outward and physical.[21]

Now these several quotations all agree on two matters, which take us to the heart of what dance is in itself: first, they stress the importance of the body, and, second, they emphasize the essential oneness of the carnal and the spiritual. In so doing they call in question one persisting strand in Christian thought which has led the church – or at least its leaders – to regard dance with suspicion so that, in the past, they have sought actively to discourage it.[22]

That strand may be defined as Platonic dualism, although, as we
shall see, other factors have contributed to this general devaluing
of the dance.

Plato understood human beings to be a unity of soul and body,
but he regarded the former as far superior to the latter. Not only is
the body inferior, it encumbers and defiles the soul. The soul
aspires to the spiritual purity of an other-worldly life, but this
means that the senses are envisaged not as windows (for looking
out) but as bars (an impediment). Death is then a happy release
from the prison-house or tomb of the body.[23] Much of this disparagement – indeed almost hatred – of the body was absorbed
into Christianity as it sought to come to terms with the thought
world of Graeco-Roman culture. This increasing rejection of the
carnal led inevitably to the condemnation of the dance which was
further endorsed because of two other factors. In the first place,
church leaders in the early centuries were mostly Roman citizens
and inevitably much of their native culture and outlook was carried
over with them when they became Christians. But the wellbred
Roman disdained the dance and so we find a Cicero curtly remark-
ing: 'No man who is in a sober state or not demented would dance
either privately or in decent company.'[24] Moreover just as the contemporary theatre had lapsed into lasciviousness, so dancing had
become a wanton pastime. One can therefore understand the ful-
minations of a John Chrysostom: 'the devil is present at dances,
being called thither by the songs of harlots, and obscene words and
diabolical pomps used on such occasions.'[25] Speaking of the dancing
of Herodias' daughter, hoping for the head of John the Baptist,
Chrysostom says: 'Christians do not now beliver up half a kingdom
nor another man's head but their own souls to inevitable destruction.'[26]

Other factors have contributed over the centuries to reinforce
this attitude. Cartesian dualism asserted the infinite superiority of
mind over matter. Descartes' view represents the most extreme
dualism of soul and body in the entire history of philosophy; his
doctrine has been appropriately characterized as one of 'the ghost in
the machine'.[27] Since 'I think, therefore I am', it is the mental life
that is of supreme importance and the bodily pales into insignificance – and with the body its language used in dance is devalued.
Add to this the Puritan antipathy to sports and pastimes. Add the
influence of the Protestant ethic with its almost pathological

insistence upon the value of work and upon the correspondingly sinful nature of recreation. Add further the late Victorian conviction that self expression is bad taste and that conduct should be standardized in terms of respectability. All combine to reduce the carnal – and therefore dance – to the lowest place in any scale of human activities.

The pioneers of modern dance, whom I have quoted above, all attack this conglomeration of ideas. Are they, in so doing, repudiating Christianity, or are they rediscovering what is an essential element in it, though overlaid and obscured in the course of centuries? The simple answer is that they are indeed calling attention to Christian truth. Ted Shawm was not incorrect when he said: 'I was a student of theology who became a dancer. . . . I did not abandon religion for dancing, but I sought it in the dance.'[28]

However, simply to say that the dancers are right does not carry us very far. It is necessary to demonstrate how they are right and in particular to set out briefly the Christian doctrine of human nature, for since dance is a human activity, one's understanding of human nature will profoundly affect one's interpretation of that activity.

From the biblical perspective human beings do not have bodies, they *are* bodies. Similarly, they do not have souls, they *are* souls. There is then no rigid distinction between the physical and the spiritual, because body and soul are so intimately united that dichotomy is impossible. Indeed they are more than united, for the body is regarded as the soul in its outward form. Human beings in their essence therefore are not discarnate spirits but spiritual-corporeal entities. In the Old Testament they are also described as flesh, but this does not mean that they are composed of the psychic *with* the physical; flesh too is soul. Hence there is no strict line dividing the two. The general New Testament understanding is the same. The body in the writings of Paul for example means the whole human being. Not only do we have bodies, we *are* bodies. There is nothing here of Platonic dualism – quite the opposite.[29]* So far from there being a distaste or even hatred for the body, there is if anything a paeon of praise for God's handiwork. So we are told that the body is 'for the Lord, and the Lord for the body' (I Cor. 6.13). Paul asks the Corinthians: 'Do you not know that your bodies are members of Christ?' and exhorts them: 'Glorify

God in your body'. It is further stated that the body is the temple
of the Holy Spirit (I Cor. 6.15,20,19), that the life lived by faith is
in the flesh (Gal. 2.20) and that we are to cherish and nourish the
flesh and not hate it (Eph. 5.29).

The equal value placed upon the physical and spiritual aspects
of human nature is also indicated by Christian belief in the resurrection of the body and in the incarnation of the Son of God. When
speaking of an after-life biblical writers do not refer to an immortal
soul of which they know little; they have in view the total human
being. Resurrection is of the whole person and the risen being may
be said to be a 'spiritual body' (I Cor. 15.44) – this is not a belief in
the reanimation of the physical particles but in the raising to new
life of the total personality. Moreover because each one of us is a
psycho-somatic unity, our salvation is said to have been won by the
incarnation of the Son. 'The Word was flesh' (John 1.14), i.e.
Christ came to save not just the spiritual aspect of humankind but
each person in his or her wholeness. No wonder that Tertullian, in
his treatise *On the Flesh of Christ*, could hymn the flesh with which
the Son of God became one.

> Our birth he reforms from death by a heavenly regeneration; our
> flesh he restores from every harassing malady; when leprous, he
> cleanses it of stain; when blind, he rekindles its light; when palsied,
> he renews its strength; when possessed by devils, he exorcizes it;
> when dead, he reanimates it – then shall we blush to own it?[30]

Tertullian wrote his work against the docetism of the Gnostics
who taught that Christ's flesh was not real but only seemed to be
so. For them the real person is the soul or divine spark and the
body cannot possibly partake of salvation; such a view is entirely
opposed to the fundamental Christian belief in the Word made
flesh. Indeed any disparagement of the flesh, even if under the
respectable aegis of Platonism, calls in question the orthodox
understanding of both the incarnation and redemption. Nor has the
church ever completely forgotten this. Not only does its profession of belief in the incarnation and in the resurrection proclaim
the glorification of the body, but its sacramental system is all of a
piece with those beliefs and with its doctrine of human nature. In
the sacraments physical entities – water, bread and wine – are the
media of communion with the risen Lord – in sacramental practice
the physical and spiritual become indissoluble. Hence the conclu-

sion is inescapable that those contemporary dancers who speak of the holiness of the body and of the unity of body and soul are in exact accord with basic Christian teaching.

Dance, then, is, as it were, sacramental in that it consists of visible physical movements which are at the same time the outward expression of what Isadora Duncan called 'the sentiments and thoughts of the soul'.[31] To the same effect is Peggy Harper's comment that we have to recognize 'the unity of body and spirit which makes the whole man; and dance is surely one of the most vital expressions of this unity'.[32]

According to Sam Keen, 'incarnation, if it is anything more than a "once-upon-a-time" story, means grace is carnal, healing comes through the flesh.'[33] How does this happen? What is its relationship to dance? Let the first word be with Lucian of Samosata who, in his treatise on the dance, says that it is of great profit because 'it brings the souls of men into the right rhythm and shows forth in visible fashion what the inner beauty of the soul has in common with the outer beauty of the body, because it makes manifest the point where the two flow into one another'.[34] Dancing is thus the art of incarnating the spiritual and making visible the invisible. So, to refer to Garaudy, 'dance reveals to us that the sacred is also carnal and that the body can teach that which a spirit wanting to be disincarnate does not know: the beauty and the grandeur of the act when man is not divided within himself but is fully present in all that he does'.[35] So it is through dance that we come to recognize that the physical and the spiritual are not two separate domains but twin aspects of one and the same reality. This is possible through dance because being a human activity it of necessity engages both body and soul.

Speaking of play, in words that can be applied directly to dance, Hugo Rahner says: 'It is the expression of an inward spiritual skill, successfully realised with the aid of physically visible gestures, audible sound and tangible matter. As such it is precisely the process whereby spirit "plays itself" into the body of which it is part.'[36] Dancing then overcomes the dichotomy of body and spirit; it expresses and intensifies their unity. Moreover every emotional condition has its physical counterpart – we shed tears of grief; we are moved by joy; we shake with fear. In dance the emotional and mental aspects of human experience are not separated from their physical embodiment but are made one with it.

This unification is in fact fundamental to all art, of which dance is one form. So according to Emil Brunner,

> In the economy of human affairs art is that function by which the bodily nature of man is united with his psychical and spiritual nature. It corporealizes the spirit and spiritualizes the body. Therefore, especially where, in a false abstractness, the spiritual element is separated from the bodily element, it exercises an incomparably salutary influence, since it reunites the elements which had been sundered. In this function, too, it gives a hint of the Redemption, which, according to the Christian Faith, will be not release from the body but a spiritualized bodily nature.[37]

This understanding of unity is also fundamental to Paul Valéry's similar interpretation of dance. In his *Dance and the Soul* Valéry describes the performance of Athikté of whom an onlooker remarks: 'She has become wholly dance and is wholly consecrated to total movement.'[38] This is to say that Athikté is no longer performing a dance – she is dance itself; body and soul are one. The body is not just an instrument of the soul so that what is seen is Athikté's body dancing at the behest of and to express her inner life. On the contrary Athikté is the dance and the dance is Athikté – dualism is overcome, not by a form of monism but by unification. Now all this is a necessary part of that wholeness to which Brunner was referring with his mention of redemption and which Christians frequently call salvation.

In the New Testament there is an interconnected series of concepts relating to salvation. These include healing, cleansing, restoration and perfection. This last comprehends the ideas of completeness, whole-heartedness, that which lacks an inner division, and it points towards maturity and adulthood. While this wholeness does refer to a person's relationship to himself or herself, it is not conceived individualistically, for it involves also one's relationship with others. Wholeness/salvation therefore embraces peace, neighbourliness, responsible freedom and hope.[39]

While these New Testament themes provide lines for a theological understanding of salvation, they do not exhaust the subject. In so far as human understanding progresses, e.g. with advances in the natural and behavioural sciences, the appreciation of what it means to be whole is extended. Consequently one can turn to modern writers on the subject of the body to gain further insight.

It is now generally agreed that to achieve personal identity we must identify with our bodies, since they are the foundation upon which a personal life is erected. Hence, according to A. Lowen: 'The feeling of identity stems from a feeling of contact with the body. To know who one is, an individual must be aware of what he feels. He should know the expression on his face, how he holds himself and the way he moves. Without this awareness of bodily feeling and attitudes, a person becomes split into a disembodied spirit and a disenchanted body.'[40] The consequence then is that we become out of touch with reality and that means out of touch with human reality. Conversely to assume that a human being is no more than his or her bodily nature is to reduce them to the animal level. Yet human experience rests upon the media of the senses, i.e. upon the body or the flesh, but not in isolation from some disengaged mind. When this integration is not achieved a number of dire consequences follow which destroy human wholeness. In the first place there is depersonalization. Simply because we are bodies, if we deaden them we are to that extent less fully ourselves. Each of us seeks integrity of personality (wholeness/salvation), but true integrity involves a harmonious union of mind and body. When this is absent, a false integrity may be sought by exclusive concentration on either the one or the other. An obvious illustration of this can be provided from the sphere of sexual relations. At one extreme, through denial of the body, there can be frigidity, while at the other, through rejection of the mind, there can be promiscuity.[41]* Only then body and mind are one is there normal sexuality in the sense of coitus being an embodiment of love and affection.[42]

Wholeness also requires functioning at one's optimum level, but for that there has to be a balance between feeling and thought, body and mind. If we reject the body and so repudiate feeling, we have to substitute logical thought as the motivation for action. The body then becomes an instrument of the will, obeying the commands of the mind. Feeling is not entirely absent, but instead of mind acting upon it, it is abstracted from it.[43] Communication is then not total, by means both of the spoken word and the language of the body, but is restricted to conceptualization. An illustration of this is provided by black students coming from overseas to read for a degree in a British university. To blacks the language of the body, and especially dance, is a natural form of expression. However when subjected to Western teaching techniques, they acquire the capacity to formulate concepts but at the same time often lose their ability to dance. It is interesting to note in this connection that the Namaquas of South Africa say of one who has become a Christian and has accepted a system of belief framed in concepts: 'He has given up dancing.'[44] Conversely, Westerners themselves, by and large, have ceased to know the language of the body – although it survives or has been recovered in subcultures. To recognize this is not to assign priorities: it is not to assert that conceptualization represents an advanced step in human development and the carnal expression belongs to a more primitive and inferior culture. Because of our essentially bodily nature, it is unnatural not to express oneself in dance. To that extent conceptualization, in so far as it inhibits dance, is certainly not a sign of progress, since the denial of the body is contrary to human nature. Nor does this mean that conceptualization is to be rejected as unnatural; it is a perfectly legitimate way for the human brain to function. What is needed is the continuance of conceptualization and, at the same time, the rediscovery of the body.

Another illustration of verbalization to the detriment of the body is provided by the man who says repeatedly to his wife: 'I love you' – and yet scarcely ever touches her. The verbal statement 'I love you' denotes and implies the promise of physical closeness. When this does not take place, the words have become a substitute for the language of the body instead of their being its appropriate accompaniment.[45] After all, as A. C. McGill asks: 'Why should our bodily dimension be contrasted with and made external to our minds? For that is not at all the case in those moments of immediate experience, when something grips and holds our attention. Then our flesh is not felt to be something outside of our conscious selves.'[46]

Finally, in this tale of woe of the consequences of the division of body and soul, we come to another aspect of depersonalization which arises from the objectification of the body. To treat the body as an object – not as me but as something over and against the real me – is to regard it as a tool of the mind. The resultant deadness of the body – for a tool is an inanimate object – is then accepted as a normal state. The language of the body is lost; it ceases to be a source of communication and its behaviour, all of which should in some sense be linguistic, becomes dumb. So, to give an extended but very apt quotation from H. McCabe:

We must be careful not to think of the body as an instrument used in communication like a pen or a telephone; such instruments can only be used because there is a body to use them. If the human body itself were an instrument we should have to postulate another body using it – and this, indeed, is what the dualistic theory really amounts to; the mind or soul is thought of, in practice, as a sort of invisible body living inside the visible one. Instead of this we should recognize that the human body is intrinsically communicative. Human flesh, the stuff we are made of, the intricate structure of the human organism, is quite different from wood or stone or even animal flesh, because it is self-creative. It does not simply produce other bodies which are its children in its own image; it produces *itself* at least to the extent of creating the media, the language and communication system, which are an extension of itself.[47]

At this point we need to link up the modern insights about the meaning of the body, outlined in the immediately preceding paragraphs, more directly with the Christian understanding of salvation and with dance itself. The diohotomy of body and soul which breaks up wholeness produces, as we have seen, a number of serious consequences. These are a failure to achieve personal identity; lack of integrity and depersonalization; loss of balance between feelings and thought and a deadening effect upon the entire personality as the language of the body is curtailed. Using a theological term, it could be said that these are all consequences of sin. Salvation, seen from this aspect, then requires the overcoming of this division, a reunification as mirrored in Jesus the Word made flesh. Now dance is a means whereby this division can be healed. All the pioneers of modern dance were concerned to liberate the body, not just in the sense of removing the constraint of blocked shoes or boned corsets but in the sense of allowing it to be the free expression of the human spirit. Isadora Duncan sought to rediscover the sanctity of natural life; she was, she said, trying to develop the dance which 'by the movement of the body was the divine expression of the human spirit'.[48] Similarly Ted Shawm declared that 'he who knows the power of the dance knows the power of God'.[49] Dance then is part of the advance towards wholeness or, in Christian terms, it is part of the redemptive process. Dance should be part of the Christian way of life.

The setting free of the body refers to yet another aspect of the Christian doctrine of salvation, here perceived as liberation. We have already noted the tendency to think of the body in mechanistic terms and to regard physical acts as the outcome of solely bio-logical processes. The result is the imprisonment of humankind in an order of natural necessity. But when Christians confess that the Word was made flesh, they declare that freedom has entered the human scene.[50] Dance is really only understandable in the light of this radical affirmation of freedom. To Isadora Duncan it is 'an act of liberation'[51] and as such is a fitting response to the God who sets us free. 'When a person feels the rigidity of his body,' says A. Lowen, 'he will know that he is not free. . . . If he feels that his body is frozen, he will know that he is shackled.'[52] Dancing assists the body to come alive through movement of a physical kind. Indeed apart from the body, life is an illusion. 'In the body one will encounter pain, sadness, anxiety and terror, but these are at least real feelings, which can be experienced, and expresssed'[53] in dance. It is most appropriate therefore that it should be said in the Midrash *Shir ha-Shirim* that God himself will lead the dance of the righteous in the age to come.[54]

The harmony between body and soul, which is achieved when both are quickened, and which is the ultimate mystery of the dance, is part of a larger whole, for it is an attempt to move in time with the cosmic love. It mirrors the climax of creation when the Word was enfleshed. Dance both honours the Creator-Redeemer and puts us in tune with him. No wonder that the psalmist should say: 'Let them praise his name with dancing' (Ps. 149.3).

Because they laud the Creator, Christians cannot deny the natural. They must however reject the unnatural. It is unnatural to feel strong emotions and not to give them bodily expression. It is unnatural to silence the language of the flesh. It is unnatural not to dance both in sorrow and in joy. Because they laud the enfleshed Redeemer, Christians cannot deny the flesh. To hide from the flesh for the sake of the spirit is to miss the Christian life, for the divine grace of the incarnate Lord touches us where we are, in the midst of fleshly experience, and that grace may be celebrated in dance.

But the wholeness that comes from God is not just individual-istic. Although to be an integrated person each one of us has to overcome the duality of soul and body, we do not become fully persons apart from our intercourse with other persons. If we shut ourselves up in a cerebral enclave, we are depersonalized. If we would live in harmony with ourselves, no longer self-alienated, and with others, it must be as bodies because that is the way we are present to others. It is in our carnality that we share the same life and eat the same food. *Shalom*, peace, is an interpersonal event, and this too is to be related to the dance. As long as we remain bound to Renaissance individualism, the dance can never be more than just a recreation or a luxury. It can only realize its creative potential when it is the expression and hope of a community life. 'He who knows how to understand the sacred dance,' comments Garaudy, 'knows the road which leads away from the individualistic illusion, because the dance is his own nature, his spontaneous and entire life beyond any particular or limited end; he identifies himself with the rhythmic movement of the whole which indwells him.'[55]

A theology of the dance, as I suggested at the outset of this chapter, must also include a consideration of its place and appropriateness within the celebration of the liturgy. It now remains to undertake this task. There is of course evidence of dancing in the Old Testament cultus[56] and this in itself constitutes a *prima facie* case for having it within Christian worship. Christians do in some sense accept the authority of the Bible and should therefore be prepared to acknowledge the liturgical possibilities of the dance. The onus is rather on those who would reject dance to show good reason why rather than upon those who would welcome it. Nevertheless I am concerned to put forward a positive case and so we must pursue the matter further.

Several of the affinities between worship and dance have been touched upon earlier. Thus it has been pointed out that both are a kind of holy play and that, to repeat a quotation from Huizinga, 'all true ritual is sung, danced and played'. The interconnection between play, ritual, feast and dance has also been noted. Again reference has been made to worship as a response to God and to dance as a possible form of that response. Dance too has been understood as a medium of liberation and therefore as a fitting way of embodying and giving visible form to the strivings and aspirations of the soul: is this not in itself a reasonable definition of worship? However we must go beyond these hints and penetrate more deeply into the meaning of the dance by associating it directly with the liturgy. In order to do this, I propose to set out a series of general theses about worship and relate them to dance. I will then follow this discussion with a further series specifically about the eucharist and similarly relate dance to them.

The worship of a divine being in a secular age is not without its problems, but the following headings may be regarded as going some way towards making this fundamental Christian activity intelligible in the contemporary situation.[57]*

1 *Worship is a response to God and a communion with him*

Few people are likely to demur about this simple statement, which is abundantly obvious to the adherents of most religions. Less obvious is its relationship to dance, but here Garaudy may come to our help. He contends that 'dance, like every art, is communication of ecstasy. It is a method of teaching enthusiasm in the original sense of that word: feeling of the presence of God and participation in the being of God.'[58]

2 *Worship is a sensitizing medium that sharpens our perception of God and so assists us to recognize him in and through the world*

This follows logically from the first thesis, for if worship is communion with God by that very fact it should increase our awareness of him and facilitate the recognition of him outside the actual period of the celebration itself. But it is important to be aware that '*how* we worship, the ways in which we express our relation to God, *determines the kind of experience we have of God*. For, to the artist, content cannot exist without form, and indeed, it is not until form is created that we can have any experience of content at all.'[59] Hence the form of worship – which in this context raises the question of the appropriateness of dance – is a vital matter, i.e. the form of worship must correspond to the kind of God worshipped. Hence we must ask: what kind of God is he whom Christians delight to honour and recognize in their daily lives? He is not the God of the philosophers (Pascal), an absolute being, static in his unchangeable perfection. Were he such, 'no one could conceive a dancing or leaping in this God's presence'.[60] A static God is worshipped most appropriately through a static cultus – form and content corresponding exactly – a cultus lacking vitality, verve, zest or joy. But Christians believe that God is a dynamic being and the most fitting response to this dynamism is creative activity. Dancing in such a presence must be regarded as an entirely proper way of acknowledging the freedom of his divine being. To refuse to dance could be to identify him with immutable stability. How can the Christian, as he or she contemplates the amazing person of Christ, be one 'who craves ordered security and does not like to be disarrayed with surprise'?[61] The free and spontaneous performance of the dance corresponds to and incarnates a belief that freedom has entered the human scene through the enfleshed Word. This freedom can only be celebrated in the body. 'Worship,' says F. Herzog, 'that is not response to God in the body is pseudoworship. Human bodies cannot worship truly unless they have been liberated to face the truth. . . . What counts is to act in the body, in the totality of our being, in response to God's unconcealment. Only when man does not subject himself to the *status quo* can the body be free.'[62]

In II Samuel 6.14 we are told that 'David danced before the Lord with all his might'. Are Christians, in their worship, with David or are they with his wife Michal who upbraided him for his seeming lack of dignity, only to be repudiated by the king?

3 *Worship makes explicit the unity of the sacred and the secular, by showing that the holy is a dimension of the whole of life*

The incarnation reveals that every activity is at the same time secular, i.e. human, and also sacred, i.e. divine. This distinction in analytical thought enables us to appreciate the dual character of experience, although experience is itself a unity. So there are not separate sacred experiences and separate secular experiences, sacred activities and secular activities; there are only experiences and activities possessing this twofold character. Thus to say that worship is a sacred, spiritual act but that dancing is a secular, physical one is incorrect. Worship is a sacred-secular act and so is dancing.[63] Moreover, since, as I have represented at length previously, dancing is a means towards the unification of body and soul, a means whereby the essential oneness of the physical and the spiritual is established, it corresponds exactly with the meaning of the incarnation just specified. It would not be an exaggeration therefore to maintain that dance is that human activity *par excellence* that most exactly corresponds with the Christian doctrine of the incarnation and as such could even be regarded as a necessary element in the worship of the incarnate, crucified and resurrected God. Is this not to glorify God in your body (I Cor. 6.20)? Let us recall the previously quoted words of Garaudy that 'dance reveals to us that the sacred is carnal' and Lucian's thesis that dance makes manifest the point at which body and soul 'flow into one another'.

4 *Worship gives coherence and meaning to social experience*

From one aspect worship is an expression of a conviction about the inner structure of reality. It serves to explain that reality to us and helps us to see how we should live in order to be in harmony with it. The worshipper thereby acquires an interpretative scheme and is enabled to perceive meaning in life in the world, being sensitized to the presence of God in and through the physical.[64]

Dancing itself is not an amusing distraction, rather, as I pointed out previously, it is an exploration, a voyage of discovery. According to von Laban its purpose is to discover the meaning of life,[65] so it corresponds with this particular aspect of worship under review. Moreover because in dance we represent something, illustrate and portray it, it becomes a school of values. Exercising the imagination, the dancer makes an image of something, e.g. something more beautiful, more sublime than he or she really is, and this enables the dancer to become identified with the image. Herein lies its ethical importance, since the experience of *mimesis*, as Aristotle pointed out, arouses the sentiments imitated.[66] So dance provides us with a deeper consciousness of life and awakens in us a sense of responsibility for our destiny and for the freedom of others. Dance, says Ted Shawm, 'is both morality and religion, because it is the supreme expression of the entire being in its responsibility towards others'.[67]

5 *Worship involves face-to-face encounters, with interaction,*
   participation, mutuality, reciprocity and corporateness

The statement by the American dancer, that I have quoted immediately above, with its reference to responsibility towards others, points the way to a consideration of this fifth thesis which affirms the corporateness of worship, together with its aspects of reciprocity and participation. In the last analysis worship, from the human side, is something *we* do; it cannot be done for us. It therefore requires active involvement. In this sense participation in worship is different from participation in a concert.[68] At the latter we form an audience and are spectators; in the former we constitute a congregation and are supposed to be performers. This fact has been fully appreciated by the adherents of the Liturgical Movement with its strong emphasis upon the role of the congregation. No longer is the cultus seen in terms of static or sedentary worshippers who by their frozen immobility either manifest the

ideal behaviour of children in a Victorian school or the bearing of a
well drilled squad of soldiers on the parade ground. This inflexible
rigidity denies freedom through movement; to dance is to burst
open these shackles upon participation, for dancing is not just a
game but a celebration and it involves being a participant and not
just a spectator or onlooker. Followers of the Liturgical Movement
have to date experienced considerable difficulty in promoting
participation – offertory processions and an increased number of
responses do not go very far. It is perhaps time for them to recognize the potentiality of the dance in this respect.

6 *Worship fosters inter-personal relations and functions in terms of
personalization and community identity*

According to Garaudy, 'dance expresses the coherence and the
transcendent power of the community'.[69] It therefore corresponds
to Christian worship which has as one of its aims the building up of
community. Von Laban understood dance as a school of social
behaviour and of love and as a way to promote the harmony of
groups.[70] Its function in this respect – and there is no harm in considering it functionally on occasion despite my initial strictures
about barren utilitarianism – is the same as that of worship. But
this means that not every type of dance is suitable for inclusion in
the liturgy. The present century, with its excessive individualism,
has seen the virtual demise of communal dancing and the emergence of an atomistic form, first with couples and then with solo
performances, especially in such dances as the twist, the shake and
their successors. In the liturgy however there can be no place for
prima ballerinas, rather we must share the same dances. 'Corporate bonds are strongly forged only when bodies join together in
celebration.' If so, re-education of the body is essential for creating
a community. Is it really possible to be in touch without touching,
to be moved without moving?[71]

Each of these six theses could be applied directly to the eucharist,
but there are certain aspects of that act of worship that I wish to
single out for special mention. This therefore brings me to my
second set of theses.

1 *The eucharist is the great thanksgiving service of the Christian
community*

Since the beginning of the second century and possibly in the

New Testament itself (cf. I Cor. 14.16), the term eucharist (from the Greek *eucharistein* = to give thanks) has been used as a title of the service of holy communion. Its appropriateness rests upon the giving of thanks by Jesus at the Last Supper and upon the character of the rite itself which is the supreme act of Christian thanksgiving for all that God has done and is doing through Christ. The connection of dance with thanksgiving is most clearly illustrated from the Old Testament. W. O. E. Oesterley says of the Hebrews that 'they were thankful to Yahweh for the fruits of the field, and they were joyful for plenty; so that when grateful joy expressed itself in the dance it constituted an act of honouring, and therefore of worshipping, the national God'.[72] He is referring to dancing at harvest time (cf. Judg. 21.9ff.), but he makes a similar point about victory dances (Ex. 15.20f.), i.e. dance gives vent to the feeling of joy and is a fitting response to success in battle, and at the same time this dance is an act of thanksgiving to Yahweh. This eucharistic dimension of dance is very clearly formulated in Psalm 30.11f.

> Thou hast turned for me my mourning into dancing;
>   thou hast loosed my sackcloth
>   and girded me with gladness,
> that my soul may praise thee and not be silent.
> O Lord my God, I will give thanks to thee for ever.

Little more need be said: the appropriateness of dancing within the context of the Christian thanksgiving (eucharist) is amply demonstrated by these Old Testament precedents.

2 *The eucharist is an occasion for rejoicing and was regarded as an anticipation of the messianic banquet*

Reference has just been made to dance as a manifestation of joy and this too is very evident in the pages of the Old Testament, e.g.

> Let Israel be glad in his Maker,
>   let the sons of Zion rejoice in their King!
> Let them praise his name with dancing,
>   making melody to him with timbrel and lyre. (Ps.149.2f.)

Joy too is an essential note of the eucharist. A description of one of the earliest celebrations reads: 'breaking bread at home, they did take their food with gladness and singleness of heart' (Acts 2.46).

This gladness or exuberant joy was due in part to a recalling of the post-resurrection meals which the disciples had taken together with Christ. At these early meals too the messianic banquet was in part anticipated. The messianic banquet was a meal or party that the Messiah was expected to share with his followers in the age to come; it symbolizes therefore the delight of the Kingdom. So, according to Ambrose, 'in joy the Church calls Christ, having ready a feast which can seem worthy of heavenly banqueting'.[73] Joy indeed is one of the qualities of the eschatological existence founded by the Spirit, for 'the kingdom of God is . . . righteousness and peace and joy in the Holy Spirit' (Rom. 14.17). The Christian's life therefore is a life in joy, and this eschatological gladness is actualized at the eucharist when the coming of Christ in the flesh is recalled, his coming into the midst of the worshippers is welcomed and his coming again in glory is anticipated.

Joy is a frequent element in dancing. In the Old Testament this is perhaps most apparent in the dancing at festivals and at weddings. But one scarcely needs to labour the obvious, viz. that love of life expresses itself in zestful and gay dance. We say of someone: she danced for joy. So the rather sober Jerome could remark: 'In the Church the joy of the spirit finds expression in bodily gesture and her children shall say with David as they dance the solemn step: "I will dance and play before the face of the Lord".'[74] Here the suitability of dancing on the occasion of the anticipation of the messianic banquet is clearly established.

Finally, under this thesis, one may apply to both eucharist and dance McLuhan's dictum that the medium is the message. Since the message of the former is one of good news, of freedom and of joy, then the medium itself, if it is to incarnate fully that gospel, must be free and joyful and may rightly take the form of the dance.

3 *The eucharist involves the self offering of the worshippers in union with the sacrifice of Jesus himself once for all on the cross*

From the earliest days the eucharist has been understood as in some sense a sacrifice. Into the long debates that this has engendered there is no need to enter here. Suffice it to say that the eucharist is a sacrifice at least in that through it we offer ourselves, and the bread and wine which are the visible symbols of our working lives, to God, and we can do this because Jesus himself our head offers us as the limbs of his body.

Now to dance is to abandon oneself wholly to the activity. This is however a form of self offering that is of the essence of eucharistic worship. To dance is to engage the whole being as a psychosomatic unity and it is therefore suited to embody our total response, including not just one aspect of our makeup, e.g. the mind expressing itself in words, but our selves in all their fullness. To give oneself is to empty oneself. Worship is a giving of oneself to God, and dancing, with the accompanying expenditure of psychic and physical energy, is another such means. Too often worship is regarded as a way to get something without any effort on our part – we come not to give but to receive. Is it surprising that so many go empty away? But to empty oneself in the eucharistic dance is to be filled with the divine grace.

Here there are three interlocking themes: sacrifice, abandon or self transcendence and wholeness. This same triad are associated in a remark by an American college girl about her experience of rock and roll: 'I give everything there is in me. And when I get going, I'm gone. It's the only time I feel whole.' The first sentence clearly refers to sacrifice. The second – 'I'm gone' – relates to self transcendence. The third – 'I feel whole' – corresponds directly to salvation interpreted as wholeness. It is not surprising therefore to find O. E. Klapp, in quoting this, commenting: 'thus it is possible for people to have redeeming experiences in the ecstasy intense stimulation produces as in the Big Beat.'[75]

4 *The eucharist is a sacrament, with all that that implies about the unity of the sacred and the secular, or soul and body*

To say that the eucharist is a sacrament is, according to a familiar definition, to affirm that it is an outward and visible sign of an inward and spiritual grace. As such the eucharist declares the unity of the physical and the spiritual. From the spiritual side we have the presence of Christ; from the physical bread and wine. The choice of these elements is not fortuitous; they represent the material powers that nourish the body. Now one of the earliest sayings ascribed to Jesus is: 'Man shall not live by bread alone', while one of his last is: 'This is my body'. Here we see the twofold character of reality, which is at the same time a unity. Bread alone is not enough; equally nourishment for the spirit is insufficient for the whole person. It is bread that both provides energy for human beings as physical entities and is also the body of Christ that is the basic human diet and mediates the holy by means of the secular. The eucharist therefore, as a sacrament, has a dual character, since in it sacred and secular are united. This corresponds to the Christian doctrine of human nature, viz. that the physical and the spiritual are one and are not to be divided. A human being is a psycho-physical or soul-body totality. The hyphenation here does not imply that soul and body are separate entities; it does imply the possibility of the soul-body split in human experience, which has to be bridged if salvation or wholeness is to be a reality.[76] But all this in turn corresponds to the interpretation of dance elaborated above and this enables us to acknowledge that dancing itself is sacramental in character. 'Modern dance,' says Garaudy, 'is a living form of communion and participation, and it provides dancing itself with its sacred function, i.e. its function of creating man. It is perhaps, in the full sense of the term, the "mass for the present time".'[77]

At the beginning of this chapter I suggested that a theology of the dance must seek both to understand its place in the liturgy and to demonstrate how it could be interpreted as a response appropriate to worship. I hope that the explication of these theses has achieved these ends. But I would wish, in conclusion, to go one step further and to contend not only that dance is fully appropriate to worship but that the church should recognize a duty to encourage dance by finding a place for it in its celebrations. There are various considerations that lend support to this recommendation. First, in one sense the church has already endorsed the principle. What I have in mind are the processions to hymn singing and possibly organ playing that are a feature of many services. These are rhythmical movements to music and that, after all, is the basic form of the dance.[78] Liturgical dance would be little more than a development and elaboration of something that is already being done. Second, throughout the ages the church has performed a very commendable function by acting as a patron of the arts. It has encouraged creativity in terms of architecture, painting, sculpture, music, etc. But dance too is an art form and it would be fitting for the church and consistent with previous policy to acknowledge that it also may have its place in Christian worship.[79] Third, it is apposite to recall that dancing was a normal feature of Shaker worship and this Christian group had no difficulty in defending it as a proper vehicle of devotion. They drew attention to the Old Testa-

ment passages that refer to dancing as a form of worshipping God
and they argued that every faculty, not only the tongue and its
speech, should be used to honour their Creator.

> Since we are blessed [wrote two Shaker apologists] with hands and
> feet, those active and useful members of the body, shall we not
> acknowledge our obligation to God who gave them, by exercizing them
> in our devotions to him? . . . The attitude of the body should be such
> as to express outwardly and assist the inward reverence of the soul.[80]

However I am not talking about the sheer venting of emotion:
that could be just self indulgence. An art like the dance originates
when automatic and spontaneous self expression gives way to
conscious and disciplined action.[81] Consequently we are not concerned with the using up of energy in an unco-ordinated manner.
From its play aspect, dance of course should involve discharge but
also design – some training is essential. Granted this and there
seems no sound reason for exiling it from a church service. Indeed
a church which believes in the resurrection of the body cannot rest
content with a life style that deadens the body. A church which
believes in the incarnation cannot disparage the carnal. A church
which believes in the unity of body and soul must do all it can to
declare the redemption that overcomes the dichotomy between
them. If this is so, then 'The Church must become involved in the
exploration of ways to reawaken a reverence for the body and its
rhythms'.[82] Is there any more effective way of doing this than by
incorporating the dance into the sacrament of the eucharist?

Yet it would be reasonable to ask, before moving on, how what
I have said is to be related to the patterns of worship at present
to be found in our churches. From one aspect the preceding discussion raises a serious question mark against the continuation of
largely cerebral forms as well as querying the production of fixed
orders that allow for no creative freedom such as dance requires
and expresses. From another aspect it would be relatively simple
to include dancing in traditional worship, as indeed is more and
more frequently done, with it replacing, say, the sermon or in any
case finding a suitable place in the first part of the eucharistic
service. Suggestions can be found elsewhere for founding and
developing active dance groups in local churches,[83] so that practical effect can be given to the psalmist's exhortation: 'Praise him
with timbrel and dance' (Ps. 150.4).

3

Sexuality and Worship

My colleague Walter Hollenweger was once told by an actress that she was not attracted to the church because 'it is not sexy enough' This is not a flippant remark to be dismissed with Victorian hauteur; it is a profound criticism of the church. If sex is a basic constituent of human nature – and who can doubt it, even if one does not go all the way with Freud? – then a church which either ignores it or seeks to confine it exclusively to the private realm is obviously not concerning itself with human nature in its totality. If worship is an offering of self to God, does not this self include also one's sexuality? If worship is a celebration of human existence, is not sexuality part of that existence? So sacred of the potentially destructive power of sex has the church been, that it has virtually operated as if it did not exist, at least as a matter for public concern. However highly it has regarded marriage, it has privatized the whole subject and not considered its relationship to the public and social being of humankind. Its worship is correspondingly not sexy enough, because it does not know how to grapple with this disturbing and explosive subject. But if dancing is introduced into worship, as I have previously advocated, then the question of sexuality can no longer be put on one side, simply and solely because many dances have an erotic quality. Consequently I must proceed to examine the subject of eroticism, if only to complete my discussion of dance, but I will then go on to consider sexuality in its wider aspects in relation to touch and to bodily expression in general.

The Greek term, of which erotic is little more than a transliteration, does not appear in the New Testament. In classical Greek it referred to love, Eros being the god of love. In patristic usage it was applied to divine love and also to human love for God. To behave in an erotic fashion meant to conduct oneself lovingly.[1] Obviously in this sense to approve of the erotic nature of dance would be perfectly acceptable to Christians. However in modern usage, while still retaining some association with the idea of love, erotic has come to be employed particularly in relation to sexual feelings, and in this respect to speak of the erotic nature of dance is to refer to the sexual feelings that it either expresses or arouses. Hence in essence the subject of eroticism is to be explored in terms of one's understanding of sex.

In this connection it is necessary to note an important movement in Christian thought over the past hundred years. Whereas prior to the present century most theological writings about sex could be accurately characterized, in Berdyaev's words, as little better than 'treatises on cattle breeding',[2] there has now been published a series of studies which have sought to evaluate sexual relations in a positive way. The pioneer in this advance was the Russian writer V. Solovyev,[3] whose work was carried further by Charles Williams[4] and by a number of other authors, including H. Doms.[5] In brief they agree in finding the meaning of coitus in personal union, as a means for building up the 'one flesh' of marriage, of self giving, of surmounting separation and egotism and of union with the holy.[6] This changed understanding of sex necessarily leads to a fresh appreciation of erotic feeling. By regarding coitus solely in terms of procreation, Christian thinkers in the past implied that sexual feelings were wrong at other times or with any other end in view – they were equivalent to animal lust. However we can now agree that there is nothing to be condemned in erotic feelings *per se*; they can be and usually are an expression of love. While all this represents a great step forward, it relates essentially to the intimacy of the private couple and to coitus in particular, and its bearing, if any, upon erotic feelings in general has not so far been considered. Yet it is precisely this that has now to be examined if this aspect of a theology of the dance and of the relationship of sexuality and worship is to be elaborated. This is obviously a delicate subject, but no progress towards clarification will be made if one rests content with cant or euphemisms.

These remarks lead directly to an examination of the meaning of lust and of the extent to which it is to be identified with or differentiated from erotic feelings. The word 'lust' in English usage for a long time meant pleasure, delight or desire. So the sixteenth-century writer John Foxe could say that he had 'little leisure and less lust to hear sermons or read books'. It is only in more recent times that it has come to have the connotation of degrading animal passion. Consequently to read English versions of the New Testament with the current definition in mind is frequently to misunderstand what the Greek original had to say.

In the New Testament the verb translated 'lust' or 'desire' is ambiguous. In general at the present day it is best rendered by the latter and, in that sense, if the object of desire is praiseworthy, it is to be commended. So according to Luke 22.15 Jesus said at the Last Supper: 'I have earnestly desired to eat this passover with you.' At I Timothy 3.1 we read: 'If any one aspire to the office of bishop, he desires a noble task.' However, the most important passage which is usually regarded as bearing on this subject is Matt. 5.28: 'I say to you that every one who looks at a woman lustfully has already commited adultery with her in his heart.' Many people would take this to mean: 'If any man has erotic feelings about a woman, then that is tantamount to committing adultery and he is guilty of sin.' But is this really the correct way to understand this verse in its context?[7]

The teaching about adultery in this section of Matthew's fifth chapter, verses 27–30, is presented as a radicalization of the sixth commandment (Though shalt not commit adultery) by way of the tenth (Thou shalt not covet . . .). The theme of adultery is not treated in the dualistic categories of the Greeks in terms of asceticism or personal purity but in a typically Jewish way in terms of one person's relations with another. The disciple is not to avoid adultery in order to preserve himself from impurity, but so that he may not harm a married union. The woman in this verse is therefore not any woman; she is someone else's wife. Next we have to note the importance in Jewish thought of the 'look' – 'one who looks at a woman'. This look is understood to constitute an active gesture animated by a precise intention of the heart or will. The man does not just see the woman; he does not just admire her nor does he experience an interior desire; he lays his look upon her and this action is equivalent to the knife blow of a murderer. Here the 'look' is not condemned as the manifestation of an internal impurity; there is nothing in this passage about the internalization of morality. Jesus is in fact not condemning in a general manner the desire which a man may have for a member of the other sex, which after all is part of the order of creation; he is condemning covetousness, expressed in the look, with regard to the wife of another. The intensity of the look and so of the covetousness it embodies is tantamount to adultery in Jesus' eyes because the man concerned has already seized upon the wife of one of his brethren. So this passage, as thus interpreted, has really nothing to say in condemnation of erotic feelings, and it would be quite wrong in discussing sexuality and worship to drag in this verse as proof positive that eroticism is necessarily evil in itself.

However, what is lust and how, if at all, is it to be distinguished from erotic feelings? Careful analysis is needed here because obviously both lust and erotic feelings have a sexual basis; they have something in common which makes differentiation all the more difficult.

Lust, in the modern sense of a degrading animal passion, is a feeling of intense sexual excitement. It contains nothing of love but is concerned solely with self gratification, so that the one who is lusted after is regarded not as a person but as an object for sexual satisfaction. In *Nineteen-Eighty-Four* Orwell's hero, before penetrating the heroine, demands reassurance. 'You like doing this?' he asks, 'I don't mean simply me; I mean the thing in itself.' He will not proceed until he is told, 'I adore it'. This is lust: sexual desire depersonalized, dissociated from love, that wants it, the thing in itself. So C. S. Lewis pointed out that we use a false idiom when we say of a lustful man prowling the streets that 'he wants a woman'. Strictly speaking, commented Lewis, 'a woman is just what he does not want. He wants a pleasure for which a woman happens to be the necessary piece of apparatus. How much he cares about the woman as such may be gauged by his attitude towards her five minutes after fruition (one does not keep the carton after one has smoked the cigarettes).'[8]

It can be said further that lust is the product of sensuality which is 'what happens when the body is driven by the mind and used as an instrument of pleasure for reasons found in man's mental and spiritual state. The roots of sensuality are not in bodily impulses, but in man's mind.'[9]

In contrast erotic feelings are a pleasurable sensation, located in the sexual organs, and are usually the accompaniment of genuine love for another person. They are, further, to be interpreted as the expression of sensuousness which is 'when we participate in the spontaneous rhythms and responses of the body and are open to the joys and delights, the pain, suffering, and stress of bodily experience'.[10] Thus, according to Charles Davis, and I accept his distinction as both valid and illuminating, 'sexuality may be lived as sensuousness or as sensuality; and the roots of sensuality lie in the mind, not in the body. Sex is sensuousness when we participate in the spontaneous sexual rhythms and responses of the body.'[11] Hence the erotic minus self-giving love is lust, which is essentially self-centred and mind-produced. It is of course possible to crush and reject the body so much that both lust and natural erotic feelings are avoided. Alternatively it is possible so to affirm instinctual reflexes that the mind is subordinated and promiscuity prevails thus promoting lust and denying true love. But when a person has unified body and soul, lust need not arise and erotic feelings are understood as the natural accompaniment of loving another.

However this distinction between lust and erotic feelings still rests upon relating the latter to love for one's partner, i.e. erotic feelings, while legitimate, are being comprehended within the marriage bond. This still leaves open the question of the erotic nature of dance or of worship which are public activities and may stimulate erotic feelings in one who is not one's married partner. Is there then no in- between, no position between condemning lust on the one hand and approving eroticism only within the circle of person-to-person love on the other?

If the desire aroused by an attractive man or woman passes over into a desire to have sexual relations with that person then the result is either lust – the other being an object to gratify one's sexual appetites – or infidelity to one's partner. But if the desire aroused is no more, though no less, than a pleasurable and enjoyable sensation, it is difficult to see why it should be condemned. What is more natural than that the beauty of a human being should arouse some sexual feeling? Is not the natural given by God, according to the Christian doctrine of creation? There need be no infidelity here, when a person is not contemplating intercourse but simply experiencing some sexual pleasure. In a sense it is a matter of degree. But then morality, as Chesterton said, is like art; it consists in drawing the line somewhere. Just as there would appear to be nothing wrong in consuming a limited amount of alcohol, as distinct from excessive drinking resulting in intoxication, so there would appear to be nothing wrong in experiencing some sexual stimulation, as distinct from intense excitement passing over into lust. What the reasonable enjoyment of food is to gluttony, the controlled enjoyment of sexual sensations is to lust. It must be admitted that such an approach has its dangers and that some people would avoid the risks involved either, in the case of alcohol, by embracing teetotalism or, in the case of eroticism, by rejecting such feelings entirely – in the latter case they simply come back as guilt. But the exercise of human freedom always entails risks. The acknowledgment of the sexual element in dance and, through it, in worship, does not necessarily lead to indulgence in provocative sexiness which is itself a hang-up stemming from the body-mind dichotomy. Indeed, despite my just mentioning 'controlled enjoyment', it is not 'lack of control that turns sensuousness into lust or sensuality, but the subordination of human bodily spontaneity to the egocentric drive of the human mind'.[12]

But let us not be naive. Salvation does not lie in a return to the noble savage where all is innocent impulse and bodily urges and only reason has no part to play. Surrender to 'bodily spontaneity' with total disregard of mental processes is just as one-sided and divisive of human nature as is surrender to the mind with entire despising of the body. To accept the legitimacy of erotic feelings, as previously defined, does require a certain element of discipline and in particular regulation of the imagination. Everyone is aware of the possibility of self-induced sexual excitement in isolation from any other person by means of the imagination. When we encounter someone else and do not control the imagination, we are allowing ourselves to treat the other not as a person but as a thing for sexual gratification – we manipulate them imaginatively. It is here that the latent pornography of the striptease becomes apparent.

In one of his broadcast talks C. S. Lewis admirably illustrated the unnaturalness and indeed the perversity of this public self exposure. 'Suppose,' he said, 'you came to a country where you could fill a theatre by simply bringing a covered plate on to the stage and then slowly lifting the cover so as to let every one see, just before the lights went out, that it contained a mutton chop or a bit of bacon, wouldn't you think that in that country something had gone wrong with the appetite for food? And wouldn't anyone who had grown up in a different world think there was something equally queer about the state of the sex instinct among us when we gather in a theatre or night club to watch a girl undress?'[13] Erotic feelings are here provoked not by seeing the performer in all her nudity but by the concealment of her sexual organ and breasts, with the promise that they may be ultimately revealed. It is the uncontrolled imagination – the mental image – stimulated by this very concealment that arouses lust. The feelings are not then a natural response to a sexually attractive person; they are not sensuous but become sensual, being artificially provoked in an unnatural fashion. There are thus two extremes of unnaturalness: the one that eschews erotic feelings as a response to the sexually attractive (or feels guilty about them) and the one that provokes them by allowing them to be disturbed in a petty way – which is what the verb to tease really means. Indeed lust is not only a mentally induced condition, it is also affected by social factors. In Europe, for example, where female breasts are usually covered, the baring of them or the promise of uncovering them takes on a lustful connotation. In warmer climates where women do not hide their torsos, the everyday spectacle of naked breasts does not arouse sexual sensations – hence what does or does not arouse lust is in part determined by conventions. Here we touch on the imprecise border between normal eroticism and pornography, which I do not propose to pursue further. I trust that I have said sufficient however to establish the legitimacy of erotic feelings.

Granted this legitimacy and granted that dance may on occasion have an erotic quality, then has not dance within the liturgy a role to play in giving expression to a controlled eroticism within a ritualized form? Since Christian worship is concerned to bring human beings to wholeness, it should be a medium for them to come to terms with their sexuality and integrate it within the unity of their bodies and souls.

According to Maurice Bezart: 'Eroticism is the will to deny death; it is the affirmation of life. . . . Despite war, epidemics, devastation, all races, thanks to it, exist, spread out and perpetuate themselves. Eroticism then derives from the sacred.'[14]

So much for the erotic nature of dance – next we turn to consider sexuality and worship further by examining the subject of touching. Simply because we are bodies, bodily contact is one way by which we relate and communicate. To say 'I love you' and to kiss soneone on the cheek can be the same thing, i.e. the former is a verbalization of what is also expressed by the latter. And yet this is not perhaps quite exact: the physical contact may convey more than the words because it is easier to say what we do not mean than to perform an action that we do not mean. To declare to a person who feels unloved that you do love him or her may achieve nothing. To hold that person in your arms, without saying anything, can bring an assurance of real caring. So Anne B. Rogers says:

> There is nothing so beautiful and beautifully human as to be held, hugged, loved. To feel the warmth and sincerity of another person. To give, in turn, comfort, strength. Words can often deceive; but an embrace – the truth is conveyed by something other than sound.[15]

Of course there is a tendency to think of touch as having only one meaning and that is sexual – either heterosexual or homosexual. But this attitude tends to shut people in on themselves so that they, and others to whom they might give it, are deprived of much support. What is wrong, after all, in an affectionate hug, a fatherly embrace, a friendly handclasp or some other comforting contact? When a mother breast-feeds her baby not only are food and love directly related but touch and love also. Similarly the French custom of saluting one another with a kiss on each cheek need have no disturbing sexual connotations. In other words, I am saying that while touch can be and often is – in love play, for example – sexual, it is false to assume that it must always be so.

Once one has faced up to the subject of touching then it often becomes 'de-sexualized'. 'It is not that it loses its sexual connotations, but that it becomes less frightening, and touch acquires new meanings.'[16] It increases our awareness of another person; it helps to foster an attitude of caring; it challenges us to be close to another and to act with sincerity, especially if we are also giving voice to sentiments of affection or love. Often we deceive ourselves and others with words which constitute a barrier to communication. Touching can be a way through such a barrier. However, to quote Anne B. Rogers again:

> The way to deal with touching is not to de-sex it, but acknowledge the existence of sensuousness; accept it. If I can accept the experience of contact, I will no longer be troubled by it. If I accept the response it touches off in me, I will probably discover not fear, repulsion; but the true content of the hug – love, warmth, joy.[17]

Being sufficiently liberated to touch without fear of misunderstanding was a characteristic of Jesus. We are told, for example, how he touched a leper (Mark 1.42), although such contact was forbidden by the Jewish law (Lev. 5.3). We read of his taking Peter's mother-in-law by the hand (Matt. 8.14), of his touching Peter, James and John when they were fearstricken on the Mount of Transfiguration (Matt. 17.7), and of his touching the eyes of the blind men at Jericho (Matt. 20.14). Frequently the touching is for healing – making whole – purposes, but it is also to give comfort, reassurance and help. It is used for blessing as when Jesus lays his hands upon children (Matt. 19.13) and even takes them in his arms (Mark 10.16). He allows his feet to be kissed by the repentant woman (Luke 7.45). A kiss was obviously a sign of affection and a form of salutation, witness the kiss of Judas (Mark 14.45).

In the light of this it is not surprising to find the kiss – the kiss of peace – being introduced into the eucharistic worship of the church. Primitively it was exchanged without any restriction as to sexes. So Tertullian, at the beginning of the third century, refers to the reluctance of a pagan husband to allow his Christian wife 'to meet anyone of the brethren to exchange the kiss'.[18] But gradually the almost pathological fear of sex manifested by many of the leaders of the early church led to the segregation of men from women. The earliest reference to this is towards the end of the fourth century in the *Apostolic Constitutions*:

> Let the deacon say to all, 'Salute one another with the holy kiss'; and let the clergy salute the bishop, the men of the laity salute the men, the women the women.[19]

The next step in the complete desexualization of the kiss was not achieved until the thirteenth century when a small wooden tablet or metal plate was introduced. Known as the *osculatorium* and the pax brede, it was passed from hand and to hand, each one kissing it in turn and so avoiding all direct physical contact with any other person. It is not surprising that other liturgical kisses, at baptism, at ordination, to the dying and to the dead, have tended to disappear. Even when bodily gestures have been restored, for example as in the order for communion for the Church of South India, it takes the form of a hand clasp – kissing is still a bit too risqué! Of course the church's worship is not sexy enough!

Now in view of what I have said above about touch, it seems to me perfectly reasonable to argue that worship will never be adequately related to sexuality unless the latter is acknowledged, and what more fitting way of doing this than by restoring the traditional kiss of peace in its primitive form? This is not to advocate sensuality; it is to be aware of sensuousness. Here a further quotation from Charles Davis is very much to the point:

> Sensuousness accompanies a sacramental, mystical view of the world, in which the body and physical nature are mediatory of the spirit, whereas sensuality implies a destruction of the mediatory, symbolic character of the physical world and the reduction of the world to pure physicality.[20]

It now remains for me to consider one further aspect of sexuality and that is sexual differentiation, by which I mean the distinction between maleness and femaleness. Sexuality does indeed determine a human being's existence in so far as he or she is a man or a woman[21] – talk of unisex is to that extent just sheer nonsense. Here the problem of the male dominated language of the liturgy comes to the fore. To any woman who has been alerted to the need for liberation and who has therefore become conscious of her femaleness, it is an insult to hear the repeated prayers 'for all men'. However often the excuse is put forward that man (men) includes woman (women), this is a hollow defence. Yet even in the most recent revisions we find continued male insensitivity to this issue and the insult to womanhood being perpetuated. Take Alternative Services Series 3 of the Church of England. In the prayers after the creed there is the petition 'that men may honour one another and seek the common good'. There is also the statement: 'We commend all men to your unfailing love, that in them your will may be fulfilled.' The call to confession of sin expresses the resolution 'to live in love and peace with all men', and the confession itself refers to sinning 'against you and against our fellow men'. Need one go on? Women are simply not acknowledged in their sexual differentiation from men. As a first step to recovering some relationship between worship and sexuality let us cease pretending that there is no sexual differentiation or that all women are really males.

Certainly a greater appreciation of the relationship between sexuality and worship is necessary if Christianity is to come to terms with modern life and show itself relevant to everyday existence. A religion which concentrates upon the supernatural and distrusts the natural inevitably evolves a liturgy that is unsensuous.[22] But true Christianity which affirms the natural as created by God and recreated through his enfleshed Son is very much concerned with life here and now. A desexed worship thus denies its very essence and should not be tolerated.

4

Conflict and Worship

In pursuing my attempt to engage in creative thinking by bringing together topics that are not usually associated. I now propose to consider worship in relation to conflict. But are not these two complete opposites, which are no more to be mixed than oil and water? By 'conflict' do we not mean that peace no longer exists? By 'peace' do we not understand the absence of conflict? Is not or should not peace be an essential characteristic of worship?

The simple answer to this last question is 'yes' and a quick glance at one feature of the eucharist will provide a reason for this ready reply. The feature I have in mind is the one that concerned us towards the end of the last chapter, viz. the kiss of peace. There are a number of references to this in the New Testament, particularly in the letters of Paul. On several occasions he finishes a letter with an injunction to his readers to greet one another 'with a holy kiss' (e.g. II Cor. 13.12). Whether or not this kiss was part of the liturgy at this early date is uncertain, although it is very probable since the letters were intended to be read out at the gatherings for worship. However by the middle of the second century it was a sufficiently prominent feature for Justin Martyr to mention it in his description of the eucharist. It seems at this period to have completed the prayers at the end of the first part of the service. So Justin says: 'Having ended the prayers, we salute one another with a kiss.'[1] This appears to be endorsed, some fifty years later, by Tertullian who refers to it as 'the seal of prayer'.[2]

From the outset this kiss was understood to be directly related to the concept of *shalom*, *pax* or peace, as may be illustrated from I Peter which ends with the words: 'Greet one another with the kiss of love. Peace to all of you that are in Christ' (5.14). This concern for harmony is also apparent from the stress upon the need for reconciliation between estranged members of the Christian community without recourse to pagan law courts. Failure to accept such arbitration could result in excommunication (Matt. 18.17) and hence Paul's reproach about those Corinthians who were going to law 'before the unrighteous' (I Cor. 6.1). Moreover because the eucharist is the sacrament of unity (I Cor. 10.17), the necessity to restore fellowship between Christians at variance came to be regarded as a precondition for communion. So according to the *Didache* (probably a second-century document): 'And on the Lord's day come together and break bread and give thanks, having first confessed your transgressions that our sacrifice may be pure. But whoever has a dispute with his fellow, let him not come together with you, until they be reconciled, that our sacrifice be not polluted.'[3] Further precision about the procedure for establishing harmony was achieved in the third-century Syrian *Didascalia*: 'Let your judgments be held on the second day of the week [i.e. Monday], that if perchance any one should contest the sentence of your words, you may have space until the sabbath [Saturday] to compose the matter, and reconcile them on the Sunday.'[4]

This proper concern for the interior charity and the good behaviour of the members of the church was expressed in the kiss of peace[5] and while this was being exchanged a deacon cried aloud: 'Is there any man here that has something against his fellow?'[6] – this was a last chance for the bishop to make peace between them.

One other factor has to be taken into account in understanding the full implication of the *pax* and that is the influence of Matt. 5.23f. This reads: 'If you are offering your gift at the altar, and there remember that your brother has something against you, leave your gift there before the altar and go; first be reconciled to your brother, and then come and offer your gift.' It was almost inevitable that if this passage were to be linked with anything in the Christian liturgy it would be with the offertory, i.e. with the bringing up of the bread and the wine at the moment when 'You are offering your gift at the altar'. Hence the connection with the *pax* of this concept of fraternal sentiment, because the kiss both brought the prayers of the first half of the rite to their conclusion and led into the offertory itself. We see the various ideas associated in a passage in the *Apostolic Constitutions* (late fourth century), instructing a bishop how to conduct himself in church.

Let the deacon stand near you, and with a loud voice say: 'Let none have any quarrel with another; let none come in hypocrisy'; that if

there be any controversy found among any of you, they may be
affected in conscience, and may pray to God, and be reconciled to
their brethren . . . Wherefore, before all things, it is our duty to be at
peace in our own minds; for he that does not find any disorder in himself will not quarrel with another, but will be peaceable, friendly,
gathering the Lord's people, and a fellow-worker with him, in order
to increase the number of those that shall be saved in unanimity. For
those who contrive enmities, and strifes, and contests, and lawsuits,
are wicked and aliens from God.[7]

Three passages from later liturgies will be sufficient illustration
of how clearly the kiss was linked with ideas of peace and good
will.

In the liturgy of John Chrysostom it is associated with an
exhortation to love one another that in union the worshippers may
confess the consubstantial and undivided Trinity.[8]

In the liturgy of the Armenians we are told: 'the peace has been
proclaimed, the holy greeting has been enjoined: the Church has
become one soul, the kiss has been given to be a bond of perfect-
ness: enmity has been removed and love been spread abroad.'[8]

According to a liturgical form in the Sahidic Ecclesiastical
Canons, after the kiss the deacon shouts aloud:

> Let none of the unbelievers remain here.
> Let none of the heretics stand here with us today . . .
> Let none allow a quarrel in his heart against any.
> Let none stand here in dissimulation or in hypocrisy.[10]

Finally, in this brief sketch of the early history and understanding of the liturgical *pax*, notice should be taken of the fact that in
the Roman rite the kiss was eventually moved to a position much
later in the service. This was partly to connect it with the Lord's
Prayer and its petition for forgiveness 'as we forgive them', thus
linking peace and reconciliation. It was also partly to make it serve
as a natural preparation for the act of communion itself.[11] So it
came to function as a barrier to conflict in the sense that those who
were unable to engage in this sign of loving unity could not go on
to partake of the bread and the wine. This use of the *pax* was
parallel to the use of the Nicene Creed when in the sixth century it
was adopted in Spain to be recited after the fraction of the bread
to debar Arian heretics.

Centuries later this same idea of brotherly love, although without its ceremonial embodiment, was expressed in an opening rubric

to the 1549 Anglican Order for Communion. This laid down that the curate was to deal 'with those betwict whom he perceiveth malice, and hatred to reign, not suffering them to be partakers of the Lord's table, until he know them to be reconciled'. At the present day we find this concern re-embodied, as noted in the previous chapter, in a kiss of peace now assuming the form of a hand clasp in the Church of South India, which has itself followed the continuing tradition of the Indian Christians of St Thomas.

On the face of it then the liturgical kiss of peace appears to be intended to ensure the exclusion of conflict from Christian worship. Does it make any sense to speak of worship and conflict in association? I think it does, as long as we recognize three things: 1. peace means far more than just the absence of conflict; 2. conflict does not inevitably have the negative aspects so often attributed to it; 3. conflict may have positive features.

1 *The meaning of peace*

To understand peace simply as the absence of conflict is to interpret it negatively.[12] But, says Yoskiaki Iisaka, there can be 'a state of peace and order in which freedom suffocates and injustice thrives'.[13] Or, in the words of John Macquarrie, ' "peace" is too often understood as simply the dampening down of conflicts which were aimed at changing the *status quo*.'[14] But a situation of oppression, for example, in which all forms of strife were held in check, is not one of positive peace. To acquiesce is not to be a peace maker but a peace avoider. This negative peace is that which Jeremiah condemned when he upbraided his countrymen 'from the least to the greatest of them', for saying ' "Peace, peace", when there is no peace' (Jer. 6.13f.). Absence of overt conflict is no indication of true peace.

Indeed true peace is not something static; it is not a condition but a process. As Owen Wingrave says in Benjamin Britten's opera of that name, peace is not acquiescence but searching. It is that which characterizes the Kingdom of God, which is 'righteousness and *peace* and joy in the Holy Spirit' (Rom. 14.17). Consequently it has an eschatological character – it is already but not yet – and this peace with God often means conflict with the world.

The content of positive peace is indicated in the Bible in a variety of ways, and in the Old Testament it usually translates the word *shalom*. *Shalom* refers to wholeness, fullness, righteousness and trust. It includes the idea of harmonious community. It denotes the exercise of mutual responsibility. It embraces too salvation, not in the negative sense of freedom-from something but in its positive meaning of freedom-for, i.e. for growth, neighbourliness, reconciliation and hope.

If, in the light of these remarks, it be granted that to speak of peace solely in terms of the absence of conflict is entirely inadequate, then the way is open to consider how far it is possible to understand conflict itself positively and to combine it with a concept of positive peace; but this can only be pursued after examining the supposed adverse corollaries of conflict.

2 *The supposed negative aspects of conflict*

Many Christians repudiate conflict on the ground that it denies love and negates unity, that it must involve enmity and is always malignant being equivalent to deviant behaviour and so is to be regarded as dysfunctional. Of course in a sense all this is true. Conflict can and often does have these negative aspects, but this is not necessarily so on every occasion. Take the case of Jesus: he was unquestionably a centre of conflict, as he himself recognized. 'Do you think that I am come to give peace on earth? No, I tell you, but rather division' (Luke 12.51). He was a controversial figure, but this does not mean that he denied unity or love or set out to make enemies, although his conduct was deviant in terms of the orthodoxy of his day – so much the worse for the establishment, one may comment. Moreover the contention that conflict always has adverse effects could be no more than a rationalization to cover one's own sense of insecurity. What I have in mind is this: those who would avoid conflict at any price and defend their avoidance by these arguments may in fact be unsure about the basis of their unity. They may fear it is too shaky to survive any testing. Indeed where relationships are shallow, conflicts are pushed to one side lest they might endanger the continuance of the relationships. In such circumstances the absence of conflict is a sign of the tenuousness of the bonds. Conversely conflict can be an indication of the stability of relationships,[15] i.e. where there exists a foundation of true harmony, there need be no worry that a crisis can penetrate and overthrow it; the consequences of discord may then be faced and they do not have to be passed over. Especially should this be so within the Christian community, the members of which should be conscious of the magnitude of the forces that weld them together, so that conflict has a certain trifling nature. Compared with all that we have in common – so we might declare – this or that issue pales into insignificance. To say this is not to question the possible value of conflict as a means of achieving change and development; it is simply to set it in perspective and so to diminish any traumatic effect, thus allowing that it may be positive rather than negative in its results.

Moreover, if we are realistic, we are bound to acknowledge that any community, consisting as it does of different groups, is likely to have within it opposing interests. What frequently happens is that one group – usually that which is intellectually privileged – proceeds to dominate the others.[16] Such domination does not of course resolve the latent conflict; it simply suppresses it. Suppressed conflict is simply not peace and often the outcome is that the group unable to share the dominant outlook proceeds to withdraw. Conflict has been averted in that case but at the cost of a decline of membership. The resulting 'peace' is only that of the surviving rump and not of the original community. True unity has not been achieved because that is only possible when people with differing points of view come together in dialogue, express their disagreements and move towards their resolution. But there never will be any such resolution and therefore no deepening of unity on the part of Christians if they persist in repudiating conflict on the grounds I listed above. Nor indeed do these grounds carry conviction as a short analysis of them will reveal.

First I have noted a tendency among Christians to reject conflict as a denial of love. But love can be a prime motive for it. The teacher who clashes with a badly behaved pupil may have his or her best interests at heart. The policeman who forcibly restrains the would-be suicide may be expressing neighbour love. Moreover it has been plausibly argued that in circumstances of oppression, the love of the oppressed for their oppressors may involve armed conflict of which the aim is to liberate the oppressors. Liberate them! From what? From their power to dominate, so restoring to them the humanity they had lost in the exercise of oppression, for to the extent that one enslaves another to that extent he is less than whole.[17] From these examples – and one could produce many more – it is apparent that conflict need not by its nature deny love nor does it necessarily negate unity – another supposed negative aspect. On occasion conflict may be an essential step towards unity, which, like peace, is not something given but something to be achieved, and conflict can mark a stage on the way towards this. Unity, after all, is a process of interaction of people in a dynamic relationship – it is not a fixed state. Within such a continuing reciprocity conflict may have a positive function in furthering a more profound and closer harmony.

Nor is it correct to maintain that conflict always involves aggression, hostility and hatred. It is not difficult to think of instances where conflict neither arises from nor engenders enmity. What of an adolescent struggling with his or her parents? This is frequently a necessary step on the way towards maturity. There are times when it can lead to excessive ill feeling and disruption; but equally there are times when the struggle takes place within a context of mutual love. However irked the adolescent may be, he or she may not give up loving their parents, and however irritated the parents may be in their turn they do not cease to care for their offspring. Conflict then is not always malignant. Such a view can arise if one regards conflict as a dire combat that can only end in the total victory of one side or the other. Of course if the interests of the two parties are diametrically opposed, then the opposition between them can only be resolved by one or the other winning. But there can be cases where conflict may be beneficial in its effects and both parties may profit from it. It is indeed a mistake to regard conflict as always equivalent to deviant behaviour and so as a disease needing treatment.

Yet sometimes – it has to be admitted – conflict will be equivalent to deviant behaviour, but that does not necessarily carry with it any adverse judgment. If the *status quo* constitutes a denial of freedom and love, then woe is he or she who passively accepts it and fails to foster a policy of deviation. Much depends upon the particular circumstances: in some, deviance and conflict would be right; in others, conflict would be dysfunctional. Much indeed depends upon the definitions. If one holds that the essence of the social process – and of church life too – is communication (and is this not part of the meaning of *koinonia*?), and that the essence of conflict is the absence of communication, then conflict by definition must be dysfunctional. But sometimes the possibility of dialogue simply does not exist: witness Bonhoeffer and his fellow plotters on the one hand and the Nazis on the other. Conflict is then properly dysfunctional in terms of the *status quo*. But it is also possible to conceive of conflicts that do not go to the lengths of disrupting an existing dialogue and indeed contribute to communication. In saying this, I am already moving towards a consideration of the positive aspects or functions of conflict.

3 *The positive features of conflict*

As a starting point it may be as well to dispose of the obvious by noting that conflict may take many different forms. It can be violent or nonviolent. It can be physical or solely verbal. The form that it takes does not predetermine its rightness or wrongness nor its positive or negative quality. So, for example, physical conflict need not be harmful: one may engage in a fencing match without any damage to oneself or to one's opponent. Alternatively, one may enter into a verbal contest, such as a debate, entirely free from evil intentions and with the sole aim of deepening one's awareness of the truth. Dialogue too, e.g. between a Muslim and a Christian, may involve conflict that can have positive value in promoting the emergence of some new truth more profound than either of the participants had previously realized.

While conflict then can take different forms, it may also be related to and studied within different situations. In particular one must distinguish between conflict when related to the question of groups (here one is dealing with sociology and possibly social psychology) and conflict when related to the question of personality (when one is dealing with psychology). In the former case the concern is with interaction within and between groups, in the latter with the establishment of self identity. In the following analysis I shall be looking at the positive values of conflict first from the sociological aspect and then from the psychological.

Let us suppose a scale ranging from negative to positive and let us suppose it has three points: conflict, peace, indifference. In what order should one arrange these three and which would be nearest to and which furthest from the positive end? Obviously peace (in its positive sense and not just as the absence of struggle) must be regarded as a plus. Of the remaining two, indifference is evidently purely negative and therefore the furthest from the positive represented by peace. From indifference one cannot advance directly to peace; there is no motivation to do so, no basis for action. Consequently on our three point scale conflict is not at the minus end (which is occupied by indifference) because it can be a means of stirring one out of indifference and it thus constitutes a stage on the way to harmony and so is to be regarded as positive.

Indeed, absence of conflict results in stagnation – a fact frequently observed by William Blake and expressed by him in pithy comments: 'Without Contraries is no progression' and 'Expect poison from the standing water.'[18] So G. Simmel, who was one of the first to draw attention to the positive aspects of conflict, asserted that

> there probably exists no social unit in which convergent and divergent currents among its members are not inseparably interwoven. An absolutely centripetal and harmonious group, a pure 'unification', not only is empirically unreal, it could show no real life process.[19]

Since the church – whatever else it is – is a social unit, Simmel's accurate observation means that if we declare there are no conflicts within it, we are simply closing our eyes to the actual reality. Alternatively, if we affirm that there should be no conflicts within it, we are saying that it should be dead. Conflict is indeed necessary for life, for life involves change and development and these can be fostered by conflict. Indeed it may be said that conflictual situations are one of the main sources of human progress. As examples may be instanced the emergence of a democratic form of government and society, the origins of which usually lie in past conflicts, and of toleration which has resulted from the struggles between denominations and sects. Moreover, according to L. A. Coser, who has developed Simmel's ideas:

> Conflict within a group frequently helps to revitalize existent norms; or it contributes to the emergence of new norms. In this sense, social conflict is a mechanism for adjustment of norms to new conditions. A flexible society benefits from conflict because such behaviour, by helping it create and modify norms, assures its continuance under changed conditions.[20]

Conflict may then be productive in any one of three ways: (*i*) by bringing into the conscious awareness of the contenders and their community as a whole certain norms and rules which were dormant before the particular struggle began;[21] (*ii*) by modifying existing laws and creating new ones; (*iii*) by promoting the application of these new rules so that new institutional structures come into being to support them. In other words conflict is a means by which adjustments to new conditions can be brought about. Perhaps the most striking example of this in recent years in church terms has

been Vatican II with its conflict between conservatives and pro-
gressives and all that has resulted in the way of *aggiornamento*
since.

Simmel himself has also remarked that conflict serves 'to resolve
divergent dualisms; it is a way of achieving some kind of unity . . .
since it resolves the tensions between contrasts'.[22] This means that
conflict can act as an integrative force. To that extent it plays a
positive role in establishing and maintaining group identity and
cohesion. One example from the pages of church history should
suffice to illustrate this. Christianity began as a sect within
Judaism, but in time it came into conflict with its parent and the
result was the gradual emergence of the church with its own
identity, norms and unity.

Again, it should be observed that conflict within a relationship is
often required to preserve that relationship. Without the possibility
of voicing dissent or even hostility towards the other members,
some can feel so crushed that, as I suggested above, they will react
by withdrawal. Of course the attempt can be made and often is
made to suppress conflict, but this is not a way to ensure either
the permanence or the deepening of relationships. Continual sup-
pression of conflicts can build up hostility to such an extent that it
bursts out in destructive fury – Northern Ireland is a glaring illustration of this at the present day. Moreover if a conflict breaks out
in a body that has consistently sought to prevent the expression of
hesitant feelings and somewhat divergent ideas, it will be particularly intense because it will centre no longer in one issue but in a
series of accumulated grievances previously denied outlet. Note
how, as the Reformation progressed, with its destruction of the
unity of the church, more and more accusations were forthcoming.
L. A. Coser's comment upon this is as follows:

> Conflict tends to be dysfunctional for a social structure in which there
> is no or insufficient toleration and institutionalization of conflict. The
> intensity of a conflict that threatens to 'tear apart', which attacks the
> consensual basis of a social system, is related to the rigidity of the
> structures. What threatens the equilibrium of such a structure is not
> conflict as such, but the rigidity itself which permits hostilities to
> accumulate and to be channeled along one major line of cleavage once
> they break out in conflict.[23]

These observations apply to the church in so far as it too is a
social institution. Within contemporary Western society conflict is

normal; the important thing is to allow it to express itself and be resolved in such a way that the social cost is not out of proportion to the evolution or advance produced. So F. Houtart and J. Rémy pose the question in relation to the church:

> Should it not be abnormal for society, recognizing the central role of conflict, to do its utmost to devise means to regulate it and so to profit from it, while the Church should seek to exclude it from its midst? Would it not be evidence of a considerable cultural displacement on the part of the Church if it remained attached to the view that its primary concern is to condemn conflict so that it can be prevented from expressing itself too openly?[24]

Such a policy is clearly mistaken and, in the light of the positive functions of conflict outlined so far, there seem good reasons for suggesting that the church must allow for conflict within its structures and possibly within its acts of worship. But before proceeding to examine this latter proposition, let us turn from conflict considered in the light of sociology to conflict interpreted in terms of psychology.

From the psychological aspect it is now generally accepted that conflict is a necessary part of growing up. It is, as I suggested earlier when reviewing the supposed connection of conflict and enmity, an essential element in attaining maturity. In adolescence the young person is often faced with two opposing interests or desires at the same time. He may, for example, want to please his parents by staying in to finish his homework but he may also have a strong inclination to be with his peer group in a coffee bar. If he falls in with his parents' desires, then he may be regarded by them as a good and obedient offspring, but left with freedom of choice he would have certainly gone out. In such a conflict situation an adolescent may launch a direct attack on his parents for keeping him on too close a rein or he may seek to compromise ('I'll do half an hour's work and then go out') or he may retreat from any attempt at a solution ('I'll stay in tonight'). In some situations one course of action would be appropriate, in others a different one. However, if progress is to be made through realistic adjustment, without either an illusory projection of blame on to someone else or self-deception through rationalization, then on occasion conflicts may be essential to enable the personality of the adolescent to grow. After all, one of the differences between the child and the adult is that between determination by parents and self determination. To achieve the latter and overcome dependency, conflict may be necessary and is then to be regarded as beneficial.[25]

In terms of parent-child relations such conflicts become inevitable if the parents are dominating, overprotective or clinging and if the children will not remain subservient. Parents in the first category – the dominating – have an intense desire for their offspring to achieve the great things that they themselves failed to do; they are then impelled to take charge of their children's lives, demanding obedience and the concentration of their energies in the direction chosen for them. Overprotective parents – our second category – treat their children like perpetual infants in constant need of being screened from possible dangers; they try to limit a child's social life to a handpicked group of friends; they fuss over minor ailments. Rebellion is inevitable if children with such parents are to have any degree of independence, and so it is where clinging or possessive parents are involved, to whom a son or daughter is an insurance policy against poverty or loneliness. Normal young people have many affectionate ties with their parents, but even those who love and respect them may have to undergo friction in order to enlarge their area of independence.[26] Nor need this be necessarily inimical to the best interests of the father and mother. The possessive mother who lives only through her children is herself in a position of abject dependency and to that extent she too lacks maturity. A conflict which liberates the child or children from this clinging relationship may also help the mother, if she can adjust, to become more whole herself. In other words, conflict can have a positive value for all participants, and its potentially beneficial effects are not to be limited to the period of adolescence. Adult participation in an encounter group, for instance, can progress through conflict – let me explain this example further.

An encounter group consists of a small number of people whose aim is to foster personal growth. The method employed towards this end is that of encounter or meeting, i.e. they seek to improve interpersonal communication and relations within an experiential process. The furtherance of this process almost demands conflict as each member strives to reveal himself or herself by coming out from behind the façade that separates them from one another so that there can be a real encounter. This struggle often explodes into an attack upon other participants in an attempt to remove *their* masks.[27] Indeed in an encounter group painful struggles are often undertaken and have to be worked through if the group is to become united and if its members are to enter into true dialogue.[28]

For such conflicts to be fruitful and non-destructive they must take place within a context of caring. Admittedly the confrontation that ensues may be either negative or positive, but when there is 'commitment to relationship' which is as good a way as any of referring to loving one another, then the conflict is usually highly constructive and liberating. Creative conflict indeed is both necessary to well being and health giving. The same can be said of the tension between faith and doubt, as H. A. Williams has recently argued:[29] without such a continuing conflict one remains with the simplistic faith of the immature.

Perhaps by now it may be agreed that conflict, despite its often negative associations, can have positive aspects. If so, then this is sufficient to allow us to proceed to consider the possible relationship between it and worship. There are of course different ways of conceiving this relationship. The first and obvious distinction is that which rests upon the extent to which the conflict is external or internal, i.e. worship may be related to a conflict between the worshippers on the one hand and those outside the worshipping community on the other. Conversely worship may also be regarded as a conflict situation in itself, with worshipper against worshipper, and as a means of conflict resolution. Observing this distinction I shall first consider our subject in terms of external conflict and then in terms of internal conflict, but before I do so I must point out that Christian worship is itself based upon a conflict. It is so because it recalls the victory of Christ in his struggle with the forces of evil and death. This triumph is sometimes presented in the imagery of military success and sometimes under the metaphor of the *victor ludorum*. So God in Christ is said to have triumphed over the principalities and powers (Col. 2.15) and at his ascension has led them captive in his train like a conquering general entering the imperial city in triumph (Eph. 4.8).[30] Jesus himself has been 'crowned with glory and honour' (Heb. 2.9) and Paul, as one of his followers, seeks an 'imperishable wreath' not the perishable one awarded to an athlete (I Cor. 9.25). So he can express thanks to God 'who in Christ always leads us in triumph' (II Cor. 2.14) . . . who gave us the victory through our Lord Jesus Christ' (I Cor. 15.57). From this it follows that the eucharist may be regarded as a triumphal feast, a recalling of Christ's own triumph, a celebration of his victory and a sharing in its fruits. Indeed in the book of Revelation there would appear to be an explicit connection indicated between eucharist and conquering hero:

> Behold I stand at the door and knock; if any one hears my voice and opens the door, I will come in to him and eat with him, and he with me. He who conquers, I will grant him to sit with me on my throne, as I myself conquered and sat down with my Father on his throne (Rev.3.20f.).

The liturgical expression of this note of victory is most frequently found in the proper prefaces. So in the *Book of Common Prayer* that for Easter refers to Jesus as the one who 'has taken away the sin of the world, who by his death has destroyed death, and by his rising to life again has restored to us everlasting life'. While in the Whitsunday preface there is a reference to our being 'brought out of darkness and error'. Many hymns too use this imagery. So, for example, there is Charles Wesley's 'Love's redeeming work is done; fought the fight, the battle won',[31] and also Bishop Wordsworth's 'See the Conqueror mounts in triumph'.[32] Moreover if my previous argument in favour of dancing at the eucharist be accepted, it is then relevant to remember that in the Old Testament such dances were a form of thanking God for victory and were also the accompaniment of festive commemorations of Yahweh's triumph over evil.[33] So dance could constitute a proper liturgical celebration of Jesus' victory in his conflict with evil and death.

Because the eucharist is a recalling of Christ's triumphant struggle, it can also be interpreted as a ritual of rebellion in the sense that it is itself a summons to conflict, a call to join Christ in his continuing battle – not for nothing are military metaphors applied to his followers (I Thess. 5.8; Eph. 6.13–17) and they are exhorted to 'fight the good fight of the faith' (I Tim. 6.12). So in the 1662 Ministration of Baptism the priest signs the candidate with the sign of the cross and declares that it is

> in token that hereafter he shall not be ashamed to confess the faith of Christ crucified, and manfully to fight under his banner, against sin, the world, and the devil; and to continue Christ's faithful soldier and servant unto his life's end.

Indeed the Christian life may be regarded as one long campaign on behalf of the Kingdom of God and against all that hinders its consummation. As change-agents Christians are not to rest satisfied with the *status quo* and must contend against what is for the sake of what can be. It is consequently a mistake to mouth 'reconciliation' or 'peace, peace' at every turn on the assumption that believers must always avoid conflict. When did Jesus reconcile himself with the Pharisees? When did Paul compromise with the Judaizers?[34] This relationship of conflict between the members of the worshipping community and the world – using 'world' in the sense of that pattern of living which falls short of righteousness and justice – subserves one of the positive aspects of conflict, viz. the way it can intensify group identity and cohesion. The extent to which conflict may lead to greater unity is particularly evident within a national community during wartime. In World War II in Great Britain there was a real sense of togetherness, of a common striving against a common enemy, and this transcended barriers of class, colour or creed. Similarly in times of persecution, those members of the church who remain steadfast experience a greater sense of their own fellowship. However while conflict can in this way promote cohesion, greater loyalty and adherence, this does not mean that the church should become an exclusivistic group – a museum for saints and not a school for sinners. Certainly such groups do thrive for a while precisely because their exclusivism leads to conflict which favours cohesion, but this is often at the expense of truth and with a high degree of self righteousness. The church should be an open community, but this does not mean constant compromise nor a refusal to witness to social justice – such witness is implicit in worship understood as a political act – which will be our concern in the next chapter – and it focusses upon the relationship of conflict between the worshipping community and those areas of public life that deny by inequality or opportunity the demands of the Kingdom.

This last statement indicates that my previous distinction between external and internal conflict is too simplistic. Inequality and injustice are not just external to the church, they are found within it. The barricade, as it were, that we have to man does not coincide with the line between the church and the world; it runs right through the midst of the church itself. Its conflict with the world is at the same time a conflict within its own boundaries. The demands of the Kingdom do not mean liberty for society at large while injustice remains within the church. Indeed liberation is a word of confrontation and conflict because it refers to a present lack of freedom and involves a judgment upon and condemnation of the present state of affairs. Then those Christians who respond to the call and struggle for liberty are in conflict with those Christians who do not. By ranging themselves on the side of the exploited, the former oppose the exploiters even though some of them regard themselves as Christians. They reject, says Hugo Assmann,

> the ideology of a false unity-without-conflict in the Church . . . They can no longer accept that eucharistic conditions can automatically obtain in a Church that includes oppressors and oppressed. An element of tension and conflict is introduced at the centre of the life of faith.[35]

Indeed to identify with the poor, in the steps of Jesus, is to choose some people rather than others and thus inevitably and properly to introduce conflict into the life of the church.

But what does Assmann mean by not accepting 'eucharistic conditions'? One is reminded of Camilo Torres. This priest-guerrilla gave up celebrating mass because he believed it to be hypocritical in the Columbian situation. However he declared that 'when my neighbour no longer has anything against me, and when the revolution has been completed, then I will offer mass again'. There is, certainly unconsciously, a quasi-millenarian tone to such an affirmation. To the millenarian the new age of perfection is soon to be established; to Torres the revolution will bring in 'a system which is grounded in love of neighbour'.[36] He failed to realize the need for Christians to engage constantly in social criticism in terms of the eschatological proviso, i.e. in the knowledge that every social situation – even one created by a revolution – has a provisional character.[37] Torres in fact absolutized the revolution and at the same time thought of the eucharist in absolute terms as a perfect love feast that can only be held in a society where love reigns supreme. This absolutizing of the eucharist is also evident when it is identified with the messianic banquet.

To speak of the messianic banquet, to which I referred when discussing the joyful aspect of dance, is to use imagery derived from the Bible referring to the feast that the Messiah was expected to provide for his people in the age to come. It is then a symbol of final bliss. So, for example, we read in Deutero-Isaiah:

> Behold, my servants shall eat,
> but you shall be hungry;

> behold, my servants shall drink,
> but you shall be thirsty (Isa.65.13).

According to Matthew this concept was known and accepted by Jesus who referred to the future blessedness as a reclining at table with Abraham, Isaac and Jacob (Matt. 8.11f.) and as an invitation to the marriage feast of the king's son (Matt. 22.1–14). Moreover the feeding of the multitude is clearly a messianic sign and is in effect an anticipation of the messianic meal.[38] Similarly the Last Supper, at which Jesus reproduced according to the evangelists precisely the same sequence of actions as in the wilderness (Mark 8.6//14.22), looked forward to the time when the disciples would have uninterrupted table fellowship with Christ (Matt. 26.29). But the eucharist, which stems from the Last Supper, is, like it, not the messianic banquet but a foretaste. The age to come may have dawned, but it is not yet here in its fullness. We live in the 'already' of the inbreaking Kingdom and the 'not yet' of its consummation. Consequently to suppose that 'eucharistic conditions' only obtain when there is absolute love and harmony is unrealistic. Such conditions are those of the Kingdom of God in its fullness – and these are demonstrably not present – when the eucharist will in any case be replaced by the messianic banquet. We have now to enjoy our anticipations of the latter in conditions of conflict.

Further if we persist in being realistic, then we have to admit that in any case the eucharist is celebrated in a divided church – divided in two senses. First, as mentioned above, there is division within the community between the haves and the have-nots, the exploiters and the exploited. Second there are denominational divisions separating Roman Catholic from Anglican, Methodist from Baptist, etc. To understand the eucharist as the sacrament of unity can only be partly true because it is observed within a continuing state of disunity.

There are then three possible policies with regard to eucharistic celebrations. One can give them up, like Torres, or one can pretend that they manifest a unity which in fact does not exist – both courses of action are unrealistic. The third course is to celebrate in the knowledge that just as the cross was a sign of reconciliation and, *at the same time*, a sign of conflict, so the eucharist can have and indeed does have this dual character. In this way one does at least face the realities of the situation. In which case it is a legitimate theological task to attempt to do what I am trying to achieve in this chapter, viz. to examine the relationship of worship and conflict. So let us continue by passing from the consideration of worship as a recalling of conflict and as a call to conflict to a further look at it in terms of a conflict between the members of the congregation, i.e. as a conflict situation, although now my interest is no longer in terms of a confrontation of rich and poor but in relation to the concept of personal growth.

I have already noted when reviewing conflict from the aspect of psychology that it can be a means of personal growth. Instrumentally it assists a development towards maturity or wholeness, and wholeness is equivalent to the New Testament concept of salvation.[38] This is that fullness embodied in Christ to which we have to attain, 'to mature manhood, to the measure of the stature of the fullness of Christ' (Eph. 4.13). But what part has worship to play in this process? Behind this question lies another: what is or should be the attraction of the Christian fellowship which celebrates worship? It may be described in this way:

> It is a hunger for relationships which are close and real; in which feelings and emotions can be spontaneously expressed without first being carefully censored or bottled up; where deep experiences – disappointments and joys – can be shared; where new ways of behaving can be risked and tried out; where, in a word, a person approaches the state when all is known and all accepted, and thus further growth becomes possible.[40]

I must now reveal that this description actually refers to encounter groups, but I would contend that this is precisely what the Christian community should be about and what should take place within it. Encounter groups emphasize personal growth and the development of interpersonal communication and relationships through an experiential process. They can foster a climate of safety leading to freedom of expression and the reduction of defensiveness. This decrease in defensive rigidity allows the possibility of change, which itself in turn becomes less threatening as innovation is perceived as desirable rather than hostile. Trusting and caring relationships then grow up among participants. But is this not one of the important goals of worship? Is not worship to build up – edify – the church? And what is to build up the church but to develop loving relationships? When the pagans said of the early Christians: 'See how they love one another', they were providing evidence that such relationships really existed.

Of course no one will dispute that the eucharist is a celebration of love, but this can be simply a verbal ideal unless there is real communication and caring for others. Worship, in other words, to be truly itself as an actualization of love must involve person to person relationships in the same way as a meeting of an encounter group. So worship is concerned with personal growth, but this can be painful. Here we must refer to one of the positive functions of conflict. To relate one must come out from behind one's façade, otherwise there will simply be a confrontation of façades and no real meeting. Conflict helps to prise one out from behind one's defences and disguises. Then worship, when there is freedom to relate and so to conflict, can be an occasion for putting real persons in touch with real persons. After all, if we are members one of another (Eph. 4.25), then worship should involve a higher level of relating than is characteristic of ordinary everyday life. The model for the cultus should not be that of the cafeteria, with its collectivity of isolated individuals. We are talking of corporate worship and not of x people in the same space engaging in their private devotions. This means of course that worship should not be either monological or predetermined in every detail in the form of a single authoritative rite. If it is to foster wholeness and to that extent to be therapeutic, it should include discussion of personal problems, thus fulfilling literally the injunction of the Epistle of James: 'Confess your sins to one another, and pray for one another, that you may be healed' (James 5.16).

These remarks reinforce one of the conclusions of my previous examination of worship as a game, viz. that worship must involve freedom within a framework of order. In terms of the relationship of worship and conflict this means that there must be the possibility of conflict in and through an open ended discussion to foster growth and through face to face encounters within the context of a rite that permits conflict resolution. This last sentence points to two matters that require further explication: liturgical freedom and the process of conflict resolution itself.

'A free society,' according to Martin E. Marty, 'cannot exist without the element of conflict; in fact it is free because there is freedom for conflicting viewpoints and forces – including religious ones.'[41] In the past Christians have not so much rejected conflict as sought to push it far from them. Excommunication could serve this end by removing the possible authors of conflict from the bosom of the church. The trouble makers must go! Compare the very unpleasant and unjust remarks made about J. A. T. Robinson upon the publication of *Honest to God*. But this is to put an end to freedom and is a consequence of viewing conflict entirely in negative terms. It is to fail to learn anything from the development of trade unionism. It is to be blind to the necessity on occasion for strike action; it is to ignore the history of the development of universal suffrage and of the struggle for women's rights, etc. Social conflict is a form of social interaction, and in certain situations it may be the only *honest* form of interaction which is consonant with the behaviour of free human beings. Liturgical freedom too requires liberty for the possibility of conflict within worship.

Yet while conflict has its positive functions, no one wants to engage in it permanently without respite. The question then arises: in what ways can worship, while including conflict, also enable it to be resolved? One of the principal means of conflict resolution is identification, i.e. a model is accepted after which one patterns oneself. Conformity to the model is regarded as determining the proper course of action and this limits conflict by the very fact of restricting those activities that would not be in accordance with the model.[42]

The application of this to the eucharist will be the more readily appreciated if we start by noting that any activity may have both an expressive and an instrumental element. A play, for example, may simply reflect people's beliefs about their own society – this is its expressive aspect. It may however also serve as a means of changing ideas about the society – this is its instrumental aspect. Worship too can have this same duality: it may express something and also be instrumental to the achievement of something. It may express community values and loyalty to Jesus; it may be an instrument to create a new consciousness or to discover fresh meaning. In either case worship can be seen to establish identity, both by setting forth Jesus as the model and also by enabling the group to gain new insights. By sharing in this identity the members of the community are helped towards conflict resolution. Peace is now perceived for what it is, that is an interpersonal relation, like love and unity, to be achieved through conflict in accordance with an interpretation of the Christian life style in obedience to the mind of Jesus (Phil. 2.5).

Worship may also be considered instrumental in terms of the

dialectic observable in life as a whole. We may note the frequent interplay between differentiation and integration, between change and continuity, between that which is dynamic and that which is static. Innovations counter traditions; the new questions the old. If one of the elements of these pairs predominates, then we can have either chaos – when, for example, change carries all before it – or death, if the *status quo* remains immutable. When integration becomes petrification then adaptation to change may be impossible.[43] When differentiation destroys entirely the previous forms of unity then any pretence of order is in vain. But this dialectic can obviously facilitate both order and progress when the forms of differentiation and integration are roughly equal to one another.[44] Thus movement from stability through conflict to a new stability is frequently possible and indeed is necessary if attitude change is to take place. To achieve this a group has to go through three phases, First, there must be an 'unfreezing' of previous views, leading, second, to the adoption of new perspectives and finally to the 'freezing' of these in their turn.[45] Conflict resolution is then achieved.

Here we have what might be called a skeleton formed out of theory; let me now attempt to put flesh on it by describing a specific situation. In a certain parish one of the choristers – a loyal supporter of his local church – was charged with importuning in a public lavatory and was sentenced to six months' imprisonment. A few days before his release, the vicar, at the Sunday eucharist, called attention to the fact that the man was soon to be set at liberty and he asked who would accompany him to meet the prisoner; he further enquired what steps could be taken to help his rehabilitation upon his return to everyday life. To many in the congregation such a proposal and such an enquiry were shocking. They had been accustomed to thinking of homosexuality as a dire sin and the idea that one who practised it should be welcomed back into their community was hard to accept. Their previously held views had to be 'unfrozen' if there were to be any movement forward. This was in fact achieved by a discussion which inevitably involved conflict as opinions clashed. Attitudes however changed as the subject was talked through with frankness and as appreciation developed of the need to avoid taking up judgmental positions (Matt. 7.1), to practise forgiveness (Luke 17.3f.) and for the congregation to be a real fellowship of love (John 15.12). Volunteers presented themselves to accompany the vicar to the prison and proposals were made about sustaining the man when he returned to the parish. The ensuing communion was instrumental in 'freezing' these new attitudes. Conflict within the context of eucharistic worship had in this way deepened awareness of what Christian discipleship is all about, while the service itself assisted conflict resolution.

This reference to the act of communion being the climax which seals the positive aspects of conflict relates directly to the understanding of the eucharist as a sacrament of unity or, using the terms of the present discussion, as a means of conflict resolution. This interpretation was certainly uppermost in the mind of Paul when he wrote to the Corinthians and stated: 'Because there is one bread (loaf), we who are many are one body, for we all partake of the one bread (loaf)' (I Cor. 10.17). What the apostle was saying is that the single eucharistic loaf is an effective symbol of the oneness of the Christian community. As through communion we are united with Christ, so at the same time we are united with one another in him. Hence Augustine asserted: 'the spiritual benefit that is here understood is unity, that being joined to his body and made his members we may be what we receive.'[46] To similar effect John Chrysostom could declare: 'We become one single body, says holy scripture, limbs of his flesh and bone of his bone. This is the effect of the nourishment that he gives us. He merges himself in us in order that we may all become one single thing, as one body joined to one head.'[47] Nevertheless, as I indicated above when talking of the eucharist as an anticipation of the messianic banquet, we delude ourselves if we think that this unity is and will be anything other than partial this side of the establishment of the Kingdom of God in all its fullness.

We are now, I think, in a position to return to the starting point of this chapter, i.e. to the kiss of peace which initially seemed to rule out all possibility of allowing conflict within an act of worship. However the result of the foregoing analysis is to demonstrate that conflict has positive functions and that in any case the *pax* is exchanged within a context of conflict. Whatever the *pax* may mean, it should not be taken to presuppose absolute love and harmony; such perfect peace and righteousness will characterize the future of the Kingdom. It is sheer pretence to suppose that it is present in its entirety within any group of Christians celebrating the eucharist.

To recognize this is not to reject the kiss of peace on the grounds that it necessarily presupposes that which either does not exist or at best is no more than partial. It is perfectly possible to have such a ceremony and to acknowledge its contribution to a decrease in, although not complete resolution of, conflict. In this sense it is akin to prophetic symbolism. Many of the Old Testament prophets performed actions that were both a sign of what was to come and at the same time a means of bringing about what was signified. Their actions were *effective* symbols. So Isaiah walked naked through the streets of Jerusalem in the posture of a war captive (Isa. 20) as an effective sign of the impending Assyrian conquest of Egypt and Ethiopia, while Jeremiah bought a field at Anathoth and thereby symbolized the eventual return from exile of the children of Israel (Jer. 32.9). An apt illustration of the way in which the kiss of peace may also function as a prophetic symbol is provided by what is known as the Trust Circle.

In the Trust Circle one person stands in the centre surrounded by a small group. He closes his eyes and, with feet flat on the floor, leans backwards and is passed round the circle from one to the other. Bereft of sight, he has to trust himself entirely to the others to support him, while they respond to his self surrender by expressing their care in a non-verbal manner, cradling him and ensuring he does not come to harm.[48] This can promote a feeling of comfort and relaxed well being and at the same time brings those involved closer together, helping them to be more ready to accept one another in spite of their differences. The effectiveness of this exercise may be shown by reference to a particular occasion, viz. a seminar on police-community relations between white and black citizens from Suffolk and Nassau Counties, USA, and members of the police force. The first session was one continuing battle, with open displays of hatred, prejudice, anger and frustration, and a polarization between the police and those who were community activists. At this stage the organizers acknowledged the need to pull the participants together in some way, and so they suggested playing the Trust Circle. The following are some of the observations about the effects after it had been tried out:

Suddenly persons began to share their positive feelings. One black man, who was an ex-convict and a resident of the black ghetto, said, 'I never thought I could spend a weekend with police officers and enjoy it.' A teenage black male said, 'Although I am from the ghetto and I am poor, I can still give all folks a chance to be my friend.' This was a breakthrough in getting the group to set aside some of its differences and move towards cohesiveness. Maybe if we could learn to play together, we might learn to live together.[49]

By this ceremony then the raw energies of conflict were domesticated in the service of order. I would suggest that this is as good a description of the looked-for effects of the kiss of peace as could be formulated. Somewhat similar in form and effect was the Shaker dance known as the 'endless chain' – this was devised to promote union and to make the participants conscious of their fellowship.[50] So it may be said that the Trust Circle (and possibly the endless chain) is a modern form of the *pax* which is not dependent upon an existing perfect unity, but is exchanged within conflict and can help to reduce it. This points to the conclusion that the *pax*, interpreted in this way as both expressive of and instrumental towards conflict resolution, does not rule out the fruitful conjunction of conflict and worship.

5

Politics and Worship

I began the last chapter by admitting the fact that worship and conflict are often regarded as opposites like oil and water. The same may be said of religion and politics: you should never try to mix them and in fact you cannot mix them. Hence the slogan: no politics from the pulpit. Even louder is likely to be the shout: no politics around the altar. But slogans do not settle arguments nor should they be allowed to prejudge the outcome of a discussion before any examination of a subject has taken place. Let us begin then by considering what politics is in order to discover if there is something in its very nature that makes it antithetical to worship.

What is politics? Politics embraces the science and art of government and so it concerns the form, organization and administration of the state, or, in the case of local politics, of the city or region. In addition to this connection with the state and its activities in the economic and ideological spheres through personnel, such as civil servants and police, politics also relates to the organization of collective life and so to social relations. Further it is applicable to particular policies or party politics. It follows that every social act is directly political in the sense that it concerns human relations, is affected by party platforms and comes into contact with the authority of the state. Indeed one cannot avoid politics even if one would, for it is a necessary dimension of all public activity. It is a superstructure that embraces the economic, social and cultural fields, as well as those of the family and the individual. Politics therefore can never be a side issue but is an essential and constitutive part of life in society. It is too a special form of social activity that needs and pursues power; it is aimed at control, established and secured by law, and seeks to regulate public affairs, often in accordance with some particular model of society.[1]

It is also possible to distinguish between formal and real politics.

Under the first head fall parties or organizations and under the second principles and the groundwork of human relations.[2] This reference to human interrelationships focusses attention upon a further distinction, namely that between politics as a branch of academic study, with all the abstraction that that can involve, and politics as a human activity. It is with the latter that I am concerned, i.e. my interest centres not in politics as something in itself, but as a pattern of human behaviour; it is a human activity and one that is social in that it is shared with others. But as such, it has surely something to do with Christian faith, or, alternatively, surely Christian faith has something to do with it. Of course when confessions of faith are regarded as matters of private recreation, they are readily tolerated by governments as irrelevant and harmless. It is only when it is perceived that they may result in far-reaching social change that they begin to constitute a challenge. It is at this point that it also becomes evident that the so-called political dimension of faith is not something added to the normal content of faith, rather, in the words of Hugo Assmann, it is

> the very act of faith in a particular historical context. It is ambiguous simply to speak of the political 'consequences' of faith, since this gives a false impression that it is possible to live a life of faith in isolation from daily life, but with the bonus of occasional political applications.[3]

On the contrary, it has to be affirmed that the God of the Bible, who is a political God,[4] is the final reference point not for interior personal spirituality but for the meaning of human experience on the socio-political level.

Now I would wish to maintain that this fairly comprehensive description of the nature of politics, together with these brief remarks about the political dimension of faith, so far from demonstrating an incompatibility between politics and worship, indicates their interrelatedness. Whatever aspect of politics one cares to pick out – government, the organization of collective life, laws – each and everyone has a moral reference. How the government behaves, how collective life is organized, what laws are promulgated – all these are inseparable from the sphere of values, but then so is worship. According to Monica Wilson: 'ritual reveals values at their deepest level . . . Men express in ritual what moves them most . . . It is the values of the group that are revealed.'[5] In other words, worship implies the assumption by the participants of a range of responsibilities – responsibilities that are to be exercised in the political realm precisely because that is a dimension of the whole of life. Alternatively expressed, it can be said that Christians look forward to a final consummation, to an *eschaton*, when reconciliation and perfect justice and peace will be achieved. These eschatological promises are however social values, and it is in worship that these values are set before those present in the context of their daily lives – which inevitably involves politics – as values to be lived. To suppose that worship has nothing to do with politics, when politics covers so much of our daily life, is to declare that worship is largely irrelevant to everyday living. To suppose that neither worship nor politics has anything to do with morals is absurd. But because worship is tied up with values that should guide us in our daily lives, it has a direct bearing on politics.

However the *eschaton*, to which I have just referred, is not just in the far distant future. On the contrary, Christ 'was made manifest at the end (*eschatou*) of the times', (I Peter 1.20), i.e. his advent marked the dawning of the Kingdom of God. Thus we live in the period of the 'already' of the inbreaking *eschaton* and the 'not yet' of its final consummation. In this tension, it is our calling to live in anticipation of that consummation, i.e. to live now out of the future. This perspective was that of Jesus himself according to the Marxist philosopher M. Machoveč.

> Jesus led men away from the conventional popular-prophetic picture, from the apocalyptic future which has traditionally attracted the interest and attention of the discontented because it is full of fantastic promise, to the recognition that the future is *your concern* here and now . . . In that sense Jesus brought the future down from the clouds of heaven and made it the concern of the everyday.[6]

In worship this future is anticipated; in worship the eschatological values are declared and partly embodied in relationships. Nor can their political relevance be denied, for how can we pray 'Thy Kingdom come', without working for those changes that themselves will be a political embodiment of these values and so many steps forward on the way to the consummation?

We are now in a position to take a further step in our examination of the relationship of worship and politics. To speak of values, from the Christian perspective, is to refer to the ethics of love. Christians are required to live according to the commandment of love, which does not mean some generalized sentimentality or goodwill but effective love, love in action, which is aimed to serve the well being of the neighbour. As Machoveč has put it, to quote him once again; 'The real question today is not whether someone takes the name of Jesus on his lips in a traditional churchy-religious way, but whether he lives out the principles of the Good Samaritan that Jesus put before us.'[7] In relation to the subject of this present chapter this means that effective love requires political involvement and that love of neighbour is basic to what Christian worship is all about.

Because politics is concerned with the organization of collective life and so with human interrelatedness, it should be conducted according to the principle of love. This alone and of itself consti-tutes sufficient grounds for the utter condemnation of the National Front whose politics are clearly founded upon hate. Nevertheless the gospel of love cannot be distilled into some universal proposi-tion; it can only be grasped in its concreteness as it impinges upon specific relationships – direct and indirect – and situations in history. This means that if it is to be effective it must be embodied in political action which today is essential for the service of human-kind. How, for example, can we cope with starvation in the so-called underdeveloped countries without political action? To do this is the modern way of giving food to the hungry, just as pro-viding a cup of cold water may require installing an artesian well or an irrigation system in a jungle town in Brazil, neither of which can be accomplished without the use of modern technology and there-fore without financial and political decisions to bring them into operation.[8] Moreover love of neighbour itself implies an ethic of responsibility. If then we do behave as responsible beings we are committed to the creation of a responsible society, i.e. one that assumes the possibility of accepting responsibility for others. With-out this, love of neighbour is vague sentimentality and the condi-tions of life at which Christians should aim will not be achieved. 'Brotherly love', affirms B. J. de Clerq, 'is realized by the media-tion of political structures. It becomes a political task and is made actual by imperatives of a political nature.'[9]

But brotherly love is also a liturgical task. The eucharist is essentially a meal; it is an occasion for the sharing of food and drink and this is intimately associated with our first experience of love, as I have asserted previously. When a mother offers her breast to her baby she is both providing it with food and drink and mediating her love – the two constitute one and the same act. The feeding is an expression of love and so nourishment and love are linked for the child. The milk 'becomes for him a sacrament of his *being* and of his relationships. In every culture that we know any-thing about,' Howe continues, 'we see this sacramental relation between food and fellowship.'[10] He goes on to state that 'the ultimate of this association is to be seen in the Holy Communion, which we may truly regard as the sacrament of the common food and the uncommon love.' The eucharist is then a meal that ratifies and reinforces human love and so provides a model for relation-ships between all human beings – but more of this below. Here I will just emphasize that by means of this understanding we can appreciate the connection between worship that embodies love and politics that should equally be the embodiment of love. We are not dealing with two unconnected departments of life – one in which love is supreme and the other where it is irrelevant – but with one life which demands acceptance of the responsibility for political involvement and for the worshipful celebration of that love that should infuse the whole. This conclusion helps us to see that wor-ship and politics are or should be concerned with the same values and with the same things: justice, equality, freedom, the use of material resources, community.

As regards justice there is little that needs to be said from the political side in general terms. Governments may act unjustly; laws may not embody the highest concept of justice; collective life may not be in accordance with what is just – but most would agree that this is not right and that justice should be the goal with govern-ment, law and social life grounded upon it. All this is too obvious to require elaboration. Less obvious is the relationship of justice and worship.

Vain are the solemnities, empty are the words, music is so much wasted time, prayer is useless and rites falsehood if justice and mercy do not transfigure them.[11]

So J. Gelineau, using words that sound like a deliberate echo of the Old Testament prophets. These latter indeed did engage in what J. P. Miranda has called 'anticultic invective'.[12] This is too well known a theme to require much support in the way of docu-mentation; time and again an Amos or an Isaiah attacked con-temporary worship.

I hate, I despise your feasts,
    and I take no delight in your solemn assemblies (Amos 5.21).

What to me is the multitude of your sacrifices?
    says the Lord;
I have had enough of burnt offerings of rams
    and the fat of fed beasts;
I do not delight in the blood of bulls,
    or of lambs, or of he-goats (Isa.1.11).

To know God is not, for these prophets, to participate in worship; it is to do justice (Jer. 22.13–16). Hence Miranda is prepared to go as far as asserting that cultus and prayer cannot put people in contact with God while injustice exists on earth.[13] If this were accepted, then it would be necessary to say of the relationship of justice and worship that the latter is only possible when it is the celebration of the existence of the former in the world. Justice must precede cultus.

Such a position is not lightly to be rejected. There is a certain cogency about it and a considerable degree of correspondence with or recognition of reality, as is apparent when one looks at any society today. Everywhere we find the presence of rich and poor side by side. This coexistence is not an unalterable fact of nature. Both wealth and poverty are social phenomena – they have been created by human beings and can be changed by human beings. However the well off are normally the supporters and agents of the very system that leads to the existence of the less well off. The rich have a personal responsibility for there being any poor, just as developed nations owe their privileged position to the existence of the underdeveloped. To recognize this is also to become aware that the celebration of the eucharist by rich and poor together can be little more than hypocrisy as soon as the act of worship ceases to be anonymous. In other words, the attendance of the rich and the poor at the same service is only possible because most services do not involve face to face relations and many members of the congregation do not know one another. However if this anonymity is thrust aside and the participants really dialogue with one another – as true worship requires – then the veil is removed and confrontation is inevitable. Then, as I pointed out in the previous chapter, conflict is bound to ensue while the political relevance of worship becomes starkly apparent.[14] So the eucharist has to be understood as a political act, referring to the fair distribution of resources, which stands in judgment upon and demands action to change unjust structures.

All this does not mean that worship must temporarily cease, as Miranda appears to suggest and as Camilo Torres certainly thought. I have quoted him previously to this effect:

> I have stopped offering mass to live out the love for my neighbour in the temporal, economic and social orders. When my neighbour no longer has anything against me, and when the revolution has been completed, then I will offer mass again.[15]

I have already indicated that I am in disagreement with this stance but I must now set out my reasons more fully. First, it seems to me somewhat naive both historically and theologically. Knowledge of the past and of human self centredness together with an acceptance of the provisional character of every social situation – even one brought into being by a revolution – lead one to doubt the possibility of the ready establishment of perfect justice and love.[16] This should not prevent our seeking to do so, but we should do so with our eyes open. However if we wait for the millennium, it is doubtful if we shall worship again this side of death. Second, while one must agree that the prophetic perspective means that those who engage in and support injustice do not know God and cannot offer acceptable worship – 'I desire steadfast love and not sacrifice' (Hos. 6.6) – there are no grounds for going on to say that those who are the sufferers under the injustice and those who are struggling against it may not engage in meaningful acts of worship. Third, this outlook fails to take account of the experience of the oppressed and, to be specific, of the worship of the blacks. So James H. Cone, speaking of the experience of the blacks under slavery, says:

> After being told six days of the week that they were nothings by the rulers of white society, on the Sabbath, the first day of the week, black people went to church in order to experience another definition of their humanity.[17]

Here there is no sequence of justice, then worship. But who can doubt that worship is possible in the midst of injustice when this is what kept hope alive amongst the slaves in the southern states? This is not to deny the importance of Miranda's stress upon knowledge of God through the doing of justice. Nor is it to suggest that the black services of which Cone writes were ideal, if worship is in any sense a celebration of life in the world. But the God whom we come to know as we struggle for justice is the one we celebrate in worship. We do not attend a service in order to establish contact with a God whom otherwise we do not know; we come to rehearse our hopes and fears before the one who suffers and struggles with us – we celebrate the struggle which itself may involve suffering as we strive to relieve suffering.

Against this background of ideas, the understanding of the eucharist as the *memoria passionis*, the memorial of the passion or the memory of suffering, becomes very relevant. The suffering of Christ was due to the religious, social and political powers of his day. Today the recalling of that suffering at the eucharist, when we proclaim his death till he come (I Cor. 11.26), calls in question the contemporary power structures that allow continued suffering in the form of poverty, malnutrition, injustice and oppression. Hence according to J. B. Metz, and he is worth quoting at length because he expresses the point so well:

> In the light of the Christian memory of suffering, it is clear that social power and political domination are not simply to be taken for granted but that they continually have to justify themselves in view of actual suffering . . . The social and political power of the rich and the rulers must be open to the question of the extent to which it causes suffering . . . The memory of suffering in the Christian sense . . . creates a social and political conscience in the interest of others' suffering. . . . The Christian memory of suffering can become, alongside many other often subversive innovative factors in our society, the ferment for that new political life we are seeking on behalf of our future.[18]

Thus the celebration of the eucharist, in so far as it is the *anamnesis* or recalling of the Christ event, brings a new moral imagination into political life and leads to partisanship on behalf of the sufferers.

I have just noted that the suffering of Christ was brought about by the political powers of his day. The eucharistic recalling of that suffering is also to be related directly to the question of political power and that in two ways. First, any liturgy that celebrates God as almighty or all powerful thereby affirms that all power is or should be subservient to him and exercised in accordance with his will. This is a political affirmation to the effect that politics, in the sense of the exercise of power for the general welfare, must conform to divine justice or righteousness. In the perspective of worship, power becomes subordinate to the meeting of human needs and so to the overthrowing of the structures of injustice that prevent the meeting of those needs. Second, any liturgy that celebrates the Lordship of Christ must have some bearing upon the exercise of power in the political field. In the past this confession involved, and still involves today, the rejection of any claim by a state to political idolatry. To speak of his Lordship is to declare his present rule in the lives of people. To confess Jesus as Lord is to affirm 'his reigning presence, loving the people towards the future realization of their humanity'.[19] But since the Lordship of Christ is exercised through service (*diakonia*), then the use of power is to be interpreted in terms of the same service. This means that 'the politics of power and dominion is to be transformed by the cross into a political *diakonia*. For God's sake the Christian cannot withdraw from politics, for the way of the cross does not slide over this-worldly reality but runs straight through it.'[20]

Consequently, since every eucharist proclaims and makes present the rule of Christ, we may agree with S. Galilea that this implies that

> his rule excludes every other rule which seeks to dominate men and that in him all men are free. . . . By celebrating the eucharist, we commit ourselves to the work of renouncing all forms of political, social and ideological oppression that are incompatible with what we have proclaimed.[21]

But how precisely are we to understand the relationship between eucharist and freedom? I think the most convenient way of approaching this question is to recognize that behind it are three others that demand to be considered, viz. 1. What do we celebrate in worship? 2. Why should we celebrate. 3. How should we celebrate?

1 *What do we celebrate in worship?*

It is a commonplace to say that the eucharist is the feast of our redemption or salvation. It is also becoming more common to acknowledge, with Latin American theologians and the exponents of Black Theology, that salvation is equivalent to liberation. As such, salvation/liberation has a threefold reference: it is an historical fact, with a political dimension, and a religious meaning.So, for example, the Exodus involved the withdrawal of a nomadic group – this was the historical fact. At the same time it was a transition from slavery to freedom – this was its political aspect. Further it was the occasion when God set his people free ('redeemed you from the house of bondage' (Deut. 7.8)) – this was its religious meaning. 'The going forth of the Israelites,' comments J. Llopis, 'is the going forth of God, the liberation of the people is the salvation of God and the history of the world is God's own salvation history.'[22]

In the New Testament God's saving act in Christ is also seen as an Exodus (Luke 9.31; John 13.1), and this means that salvation is incarnate in the world of human liberation. 'For freedom Christ has set us free; stand fast therefore, and do not submit again to a yoke of slavery' (Gal. 5.1). Hence the statement issued by the Bangkok Assembly:

> Within the comprehensive notion of salvation, we see the saving work in four social dimensions:
>
> (*a*) Salvation works in the struggle for economic justice against the exploitation of people by people.
>
> (*b*) Salvation works in the struggle for human dignity against political oppression of human beings by their fellow men.
>
> (*c*) Salvation works in the struggle for solidarity against the alienation of person from person.
>
> (*d*) Salvation works in the struggle for hope against despair in personal life.[23]

So we arrive at an answer to our first question: what do we celebrate in worship? We celebrate freedom. The eucharist is the celebration of freedom because it is the feast of redemption and of the resurrection of Christ whereby the power of death was broken and all that is death dealing was brought under judgment. To be liberated is to know indeed what the resurrection from the dead is all about.

> When God raised Jesus from the dead [so James Cone] he affirmed that Jesus' historical identity with the freedom of the poor was in fact divinity taking on humanity for the purpose of liberating human beings from sin and death. It is within this context that the resurrection is a *political* event. The politics of the resurrection is found in its gift of freedom to the poor and helpless. Being granted freedom while they are still poor, they can know that their poverty is a contrived

phenomenon, traceable to the rich and powerful of this world. This new knowledge about themselves and the world, as disclosed in and through the resurrection, requires that the poor practise political activity against the social and economic structures that make them poor. Not to fight is to deny the freedom of the resurrection. It is to deny the reality of Christ's presence with us in the struggle to liberate the slaves from bondage. This is the political side of the resurrection of Jesus.[24]

So we celebrate here and now the transition from slavery to liberty in the risen Christ, which is an historical fact, with a political dimension, and a religious meaning. This then challenges us to engage in a continuing assault on the actual injustices that mar our society.[25] Here the eucharist understood in relation to politics joins the previous consideration of it in connection with conflict when we saw it as a ritual of rebellion summoning to conflict.

2 Why should we celebrate?

While Christians are at one with all those who work for emancipation, this does not mean that there is no difference between the Christian and the non-Christian. A group of believers struggling to further the process of liberation is not simply and solely a political cell; it is not just this because it is based upon God's action and promise in Jesus which is celebrated in the liturgy. Hence E. Schillebeeckx quite rightly asserts that 'all Christian praxis is founded on faith in God and the critical community that does not express and celebrate this faith liturgically is cutting itself off from the source from which it draws its strength to live and work for freedom precisely as a Christian community'.[26]

We celebrate the Liberator in order to affirm, rejoice in and discover the possibility of the freedom that God offers to all. So as through worship we envisage new forms of social existence – what H. Cox has called engaging in 'political fantasy'[27] – we discover that freedom is not just a dream, nor something that awaits us only in the sky when we die. 'By providing anticipation and room for alternatives and experiments, feasts and acts of worship bring a hitherto unknown freedom into unfree life', so J. Moltmann.[28] We eucharistize the God of hope so that the longed-for future impinges on the present act of worship to spur us on in renewed hope to assault the fetters of unfreedom.

3 *How should we celebrate?*

How is the political reference of freedom to be liturgically embodied? All acts of worship have two main aspects and these are usually designated ritual and ceremonial. According to strict ecclesiastical usage ritual refers to the words and ceremonial to the actions. Obviously the two are very closely related, e.g. the words are often commentaries on the actions. Both however do reveal the influence of political attitudes and neither can be really neutral. So when an authoritarian outlook is prevalent, the language will convey ideas of dependence, obedience, etc., and the actions and structure of the assembly will also express inequality. If, on the other hand, an egalitarian outlook is to the fore, this too will be reflected in both ritual and ceremonial.[29] However despite this close interplay, I propose to consider these two separately for clarity of exposition, dealing first with the contents or words and then with the form or actions.

To speak of the contents of a service related to politics is to consider certain themes and attitudes that require to be expressed. It has to be admitted that many of these are most noticeable for their absence from both traditional and revised fixed liturgies. So it is to be remarked that much of Christian worship in the past has been essentially ahistorical. According to J. L. Segundo, the mass

> is characterized by unvarying liturgical elements, pre-established readings, an unchanging eucharistic service, and the eternal return of the same feasts on the yearly liturgical calendar. In short, it constitutes the polar opposite of a religion based upon historical sensitivity. Except in minor details, the Sunday mass remains the same before and after a general disaster, an international crisis and a thoroughgoing revolution.[30]

When this is the case the political relevance of worship is obscured as is the historical character of the divinity we celebrate, whose interest is not in things or beings non-temporal but in us creatures of space and time. Indeed worship is not to protect us from the risks and responsibilities of history.[31] It should be a sign of the deepening of our interpretation of and commitment to the historical process geared towards human liberation.[32] The eucharist must then be earthed in contemporary history, while still recalling the past of Christ's advent and anticipating God's future. The corollary of this, as far as historical and therefore political themes are concerned, is that Christian worship has to be partisan. But then it always has been and indeed cannot be otherwise – neutrality is an unsubstantial myth. In general Christian worship has been partisan by supporting the *status quo* and promoting an attitude of submission to those in authority.[33] However once the question of freedom is raised, then this perspective becomes highly doubtful. Admittedly there may be occasions when support for the secular power is called for and the liturgy can have a stabilizing effect in this respect. But when worship reinforces unjust authority and delays change,[34] it is clearly denying its true character as a celebration of freedom. In such circumstances, support of the *status quo* by passive acquiescence is the subordination of the transcendent to human security. In contrast to this one has to accept, with James Cone, that 'God is not simply the God of politics but the God of the politics of the oppressed, liberating them from bondage'.[35]

There is however a dilemma that faces anyone who seeks to devise a politically relevant liturgy. Either it becomes no more than a preaching of universal brotherly love or it affirms one or other course of political action.[36] The first is necessarily abstract, platitudinous and otiose. Everyone will agree that love ought to be universalized, but such a proposition means absolutely nothing and can mean nothing unless it is related to specific situations. Yet as soon as it is so related it necessarily involves one or other course of political action. But this second possibility is not to be avoided by the Christian who takes seriously the establishment of freedom. It may result in conflict, but conflict, as I argued in the previous chapter, is not necessarily unfruitful.

Yet there is another danger and that is that the act of worship may become a form of manipulation. In other words, the service instead of having political relevance may become politicized in the sense that it is employed for specific political ends to propagate certain political attitudes and to indoctrinate in an authoritarian manner. If that happens then the act of worship will in fact deny the liberation upon which it may claim to be based. The danger of this degeneration may be avoided if two safeguards are observed. First, the service should be prepared in advance by the worshipping group itself, in which case its members are scarcely likely to seek to manipulate themselves. Second, the possibility of expressing political differences must be a real one so that the freedom of everyone is preserved. In this sense the protest masses celebrated in South America, with the intention of helping the participants to become aware of their state of oppression, did not go beyond the bounds of legitimate advocacy as distinct from dictatorial propaganda.

There is one further theme bearing upon our subject that merits attention before we pass from content to form and that is the subject of the Kingdom of God. According to M. Machoveč, 'because Jesus and his first disciples did not draw a line between this world and the "other" world, the consequences of his reflections about the Kingdom of God concern this world, with its history, politics, social situations, and the real longings of real men for their earthly future.'[37] There is then a link between the Kingdom and politics. There is also a link between the Kingdom and the eucharist, in that the latter is a foretaste of the former. Indeed, the eucharist, as we have seen, is an anticipation of the messianic banquet, of that feast that symbolizes the bliss and fellowship of the fully consummated reign of God. But the rule or Kingdom of God involves social relations which are themselves the subject of politics. Thus we see that politics, Kingdom and eucharist constitute an interconnected trio. This enables me to state that the eucharist is a political act because it in its turn makes a statement about human nature and about the principles and groundwork of human interrelatedness. So it speaks of equality, of a concern for reconciliation that is the opposite of individual and social alienation. It is intended to be an embodiment and expression of efficacious love and therefore of justice in terms of freedom and material welfare. But to proclaim these things is vain unless there is a consistent effort to have them actualized in society at large and this requires their embodiment in a political programme. Moreover the eucharist is the celebration of Christian hope and therefore sets forth the dominant eschatological direction within which specific political action for the implementation of justice etc. is to be planned. While the *eschaton* or ultimate relativizes the here and now or penultimate, it also provides a standard of reference for dealing with it and for making concrete plans towards greater freedom.

Next we turn to form. Since we are moving from words to actions, we need to stress again that talking about the efficacy of love does not automatically solve anything. Worship should be a ratification and reinforcement of love, just as politics should be the mediation of love, but love will not abound and flow over into political activity if it is merely a question of words. Love demands face to face relations and interaction between the members of the worshipping group. Dorothee Soelle, speaking of theology, says that the question for it is 'whether it makes men more capable of love, whether it encourages or obstructs the liberation of the individual and the community'.[38] The same can be said of worship. It is or should be about being-for-others: first within the limited bounds of the group and then beyond them to the world at large. If the eucharist does not foster being-for-others, of what use is it? Is it not a denial of its essential being, without which it ceases to have any reality? The same can be said of liberation.

I have stated *ad nauseam* that worship is a feast of liberation – but is it? Do we feel liberated as we worship? That we are free is not true because it is declared. It is only true when it becomes a concrete social reality. We are free in worship only if our worship is itself liberating. We should be more interested in worship being liberative than in its asserting liberation. Freedom should refer not so much to content as to the method by which we worship. If worship fails to liberate us, it is idle to endorse words that keep on protesting that we are free.

To be a Christian is to be on the way towards the goal of total freedom. But this way will only lead to the goal if it is itself a fore-taste of that freedom. 'The goal,' says Jürgen Moltmann, 'is only made credible by the path to it.'[38] He continues: 'the liberating feast of the resurrection of Christ stands between the slavery of the past and the coming life in freedom. It manifests the joy of free-dom, since there is no other way in which the experience of free-dom can be comprehended.'[40] In other words, truly to worship is to experience liberation, to know what freedom is and so to keep alive the hope of freedom – like the enslaved blacks in the southern states – as we struggle to actualize through politics that which we already know in part through worship. Freedom in worship calls in question every limitation of freedom in everyday life and it then becomes an imperative to political action. Worship has now to be at the service of liberating human relationships. So Gelineau declares: 'The celebration will show forth its political power only if the relations between the participants themselves constitute models which induce liberation.'[41] So if the Christian congregation is to be a sign of the future society, it must take the shape of the future, and this means that it will erase the divisions that plague society and are a denial of love. 'The composition of the group bespeaks a commitment to an open society; its very existence becomes a sacrament to the world.'[42] As it worships and so functions as a sign of the possibility of human beings loving one another, the congregation is provided with an impetus for the transformation of the entire human society. In other words, the eucharist is to be a hopeful sign of a future political reality, viz. of a community where equality, justice, etc. are supreme.[43]

Yet Christian worship will not be a true sign and free association within the context of worship will be impeded if the only liturgical diet available is that of a fixed liturgy. I have elsewhere criticized at length the present policy of many churches of revising liturgies to produce yet more fixed liturgies,[44] and I need only emphasize here that a fixed liturgy is bound to be dependency forming. It does not allow for creativity; it does not permit freedom; it ceases to be a game and becomes the creature of rules; it cannot be liberating; it tends to be ahistorical and so distanced from politics; it limits any freedom of choice. Of course in daily life many, though not all, people have a certain degree of choice – they make decisions and respond to what they hear. But in a service where all is predetermined or where one person performs a dominant role, freedom is largely reduced to nothing and the discrepancy between it and daily life is blatantly obvious. All this means that worship, if it is to have a political relevance in terms of justice, must become unfrozen and a greater part must be played by the laity in its creation and continuance.

We have now looked at ritual (words) and ceremonial (action) – using the latter to refer to how the service is arranged – and I have given some general indications of an approach to the way to celebrate. In the remaining final paragraphs I want to take certain elements normally found in Christian worship and consider briefly the political dimension of each. The seven elements I have chosen are the confession of sin, the Bible readings, the sermon, prayer, the offertory, communion and dialogue.

1 *Confession* When one looks at the acquisitive society which capitalism has produced in the West, it is difficult to disagree with Dorothee Soelle's verdict that the political and economic situation in which we live *compels* many to commit sin. Under capitalism the

business man or industrialist is required – more or less come what may – to achieve success by increasing profits and outstripping his rivals. His ethic can be no more that a few guide lines to help in this Catch 22 situation. Yet what is needed is not some watered down moral imperative, which operates to dull the conscience, but a transformation of society so that maximization of profits and the increase in the GNP are not made the supreme goals. In such a context the sinner is one who almost inescapably either collaborates with the system or is apathetic towards it and so in fact supports it.[45] In either case confession of sin within worship should embrace all this and so come to have a political reference. No longer then would there be much point in vague statements about straying like sheep nor in admissions of so-called private sins. Sin finds its expression just as much in the economic and social spheres. It shows a lack of moral perception not to be aware of this and not to see that it is therefore related to confession.

2 *Bible Readings* Having drawn freely in this chapter on the Bible to illustrate how, for example, to know God is to act justly, how salvation/liberation has an unavoidable political aspect, how love of neighbour must be actualized in the political arena, etc., it should not be necessary to point out how time and again the lections relate directly to politics. Even if the direct relation is not always immediately apparent, then it can be made so through the next element, i.e. in the sermon.

3 *Sermon* Because, as I have argued above, Christian salvation is incarnate in the work of human liberation, the function of the sermon should be to point out the present working of God in history in terms of freedom.

Of course the sermon often takes the form of an exegesis of one of the lections. The method adopted in the past has been usually to apply the text to the problems of the individual or of his or her family. Seldom have the texts been related to the political situation, But why should they not be so? Is it not part of the task of biblical interpretation to relate the historico-critical consciousness to the contemporary political scene?

The sermon too can be regarded as a proclamation of the gospel. As such it may be a powerful tool for what the Latin Americans call conscientization. Conscientization – an ugly word but one that is here to stay – means awareness-building; it is an opening of the eyes to the present situation. It is an awakening of the critical consciousness which produces a feeling of social discontent as, through the gospel, the discrepancy between what is and what may be becomes apparent. The gospel declares the reality of the present is to be found in its potentialities for the future, but in the very process of pointing to this reality the gospel lays bear self deception, rejects fatalism and requires the hearers to become agents of change. What really motivates Christians after all to participate in the process of liberation of oppressed people, comments G. G. Merino, is 'the radical incompatibility of the demands of the gospel with an unjust and alienated society'.[46]

4 *Prayer* Prayer is not some magical formula or incantation; it is not simply a matter of uttering a petition and then leaving the outcome to God. To pray for something – peace, the ending of injustice, the overthrow of racism – is to commit oneself to its realization. So Karl Barth said that 'a prayer in which one would avoid or wished to avoid such a summons would be a worthless, useless one'.[47] This understanding of the practice of prayer, that it involves a commitment to action to achieve that for which one prays, is endorsed by the bishops of the Haut-Volta:

> The Our Father compels us to recognize that we have a role in the world. To ask God that his Kingdom may come while doing nothing to further the rule of love in the world is to mock God. Would it not make a mockery of ourselves, our brothers and of God himself if we were to ask for our daily bread without attempting – in our situation – to resolve the economic problems which we face in our country? Would it not make a mockery of ourselves, our brothers and of God himself if we were to ask to be delivered from evil and at the same time did not strive to develop our political and social institutions which provide the conditions for internal and external peace in the future?[48]

Need one say more? Prayer and political action are two sides of the same coin.

5 *Offertory* The presentation of bread and wine in the eucharist, for which the technical term is the offertory, is concerned with the whole economic and industrial life of humankind, and therefore with politics. We do not offer just grain and grapes, but bread and wine which are a microcosm of our present industrial system at the national and international levels. The corn and the grapes have been cultivated and harvested in diverse quarters of the globe

with implements that have been forged of metal mined in different areas and powered by all kinds of fuel. They have been transported by a vast system of shipping, imported by means of an elaborate method of international exchange under the scrutiny of customs and excise organizations; they have been processed by a multitude of related trades and finally distributed by another network of transport and retailing. Each loaf, each cup of wine, represents the unity of industrial and economic effort. The differentiation, which is characteristic of modern secularized society, finds its unity in a single loaf of bread and a cup of wine.[49]

But the offertory also expresses fundamental Christian insights about these activities. It affirms, first, that they are all subordinate to God and are therefore to be ordered in accordance with his purpose, i.e. politics must be devoted to humanization and social and economic life must be structured in terms of effective love. In the second place, in so far as the offertory involved originally and still involves the giving of more than is actually required for each eucharist, the surplus being for the poor, it declares and embodies commitment to the underprivileged. It is a way of manifesting solidarity with the poor and such solidarity 'implies the transformation of the existing social order'.[50] Indeed the offering of food and drink to God today is a political act because it only has any meaning if it points towards the changing of a society organized for the benefit of a few who appropriate the value of the work done by the many.

6 *Communion*   The political meaning of the act of communion is closely related to that of the offertory just outlined. According to R. Howe:

> since our Lord used bread and wine to be the external signs of his love and life, it is implicit in this act that all manufactured things may be expressive instruments of love and life. In this way, the sacrament of the Holy Communion speaks to the way in which persons possess and use the things that men make.[51]

This possession and use are to be understood in relation to communion, which is one way of translating the Greek word *koinonia*. That term, as used in the New Testament, also includes the ideas of fellowship, participation and sharing.[52] Communion, in other words, is about the fair distribution of resources – how bitter Paul was against those who did not appreciate this (I Cor. 11.21) – and therefore to communicate is to pronounce a judgment upon structures of oppression or upon oneself if one either supports those structures or passively acquiesces in their continuance.

But fellowship and sharing also relate to solidarity – we are members one of another (Rom. 12.5). Through the act of communion we are united with Christ and in him with one another. Yet this oneness in Christ does not refer simply to the local congregation. All Christians are one in him through their sharing in his eucharistic body. This should have its effects in the political field just as our political actions have an influence upon our worship. All the wars, for instance, that Christians have waged against each other over the centuries have been sins against the fellowship of the Lord's Supper. Equally the misery of fellow Christians in the Third World is misery within the one body, so that every communion in Western affluent society has to do with overseas aid.[53] Yet it is not only our fellow Christians that concern us. Our communion with Christ carries with it oneness with all the hungry and thirsty through whom we meet him in the world – 'Lord, when did we see thee hungry and feed thee, or thirsty and give thee drink? . . . As you did it to one of the least of these my brethren, you did it to me' (Matt. 25.37, 39). This solidarity with the poor and with the exploited is thereby intensified and their needs become our concerns. This solidarity means realizing the injustice upon which an exploiting social order is built. This solidarity involves action against that which gives rise to the oppression. To communicate is not to swallow a spiritual sedative but to be drawn into the dynamic action of Christ through the Spirit in the world to break down and to build up (Eccles. 3.3) – to break down structures of oppression and to lay the foundation of a responsible and caring society that may be a true foretaste of the Kingdom of God.

7 *Dialogue* This is not an element in the traditional liturgies, but I have argued elsewhere that it should be a normal part of any act of worship that involves face to face relations. The subject of the dialogue will obviously differ from occasion to occasion, but there will be times when it is right and proper that it should include social and political criticism.[54]

Worship and politics? I trust that this chapter will have disposed of any persisting belief that they need be incompatible. Worship and politics are two ways of acting in God's world and they interpenetrate one another. Worship can provide guide lines for political action, while politics can put into effect that love which is at the centre of the eucharist. But self-regarding policies deny that eucharistic love and eucharistic celebrations divorced from efficacious love in the political field are so many vain feasts akin to those that, according to Isaiah, God hates (Isa. 1.14). Yet worship can foster a vision of the Kingdom of God, of human interrelatedness, and then political involvement is needed to further the process of making that vision a reality.

6

Laughter and Worship

There is laughter in the vestibule of the temple, the echo of laughter in the temple itself, but only faith and prayer, and no laughter, in the holy of holies.[1]

If these words of Reinhold Niebuhr were considered to be un-questionably true, the title of this chapter would be meaningless. His remark excludes laughter from worship. Moreover much of what I have written in previous chapters would be called in question. To consider worship as play but to exclude all laughter is to impoverish the entire concept. To review the possibility of litur-gical dance and confine it to a uniform solemnity is to deny that joy of which laughter and dance itself are frequently the appro-priate expressions. To argue that worship and conflict may be associated but with humour absent is to surrender a valid safety valve that can provide an institutionalized outlet for hostility and discontent. To discuss politics in the context of worship and not to question the seriousness of the debate with a smile is to run the risk of pomposity. Indeed if worship be the offering of the whole self to God, one is offering a dehumanized self when it is minus laughter, since wit and humour are essential components of being human.

Fortunately, however, the pronouncements of any theologian – even one of the stature of Niebuhr – are not to be absolutized. They have to be approached with that comic spirit that calls in question any pretension to go beyond what is finite and contingent. We theologians have to admit that much of what we say today may be demonstrated to be nonsense tomorrow. We must not seek to avoid the humility that refuses to allow us to take ourselves too seriously. We need to share something of that spirit that was revealed by Karl Barth when he said of his theological *summa*:

The angels laugh at old Karl. They laugh at him because he tries to grasp the truth about God in a book of Dogmatics. They laugh at the fact that volume follows volume and each is thicker than the previous one. As they laugh, they say to one another: 'Look! Here he comes now with his little push cart full of volumes of the Dogmatics!'[2]

However, if Niebuhr is not to be allowed the last word, we must, paradoxically enough, undertake in all seriousness an examination of laughter and worship in order to determine what their relationship may be. The most penetrating analysis, in recent years, of humour as giving rise to laughter is that which is contained in the opening chapters of Arthur Koestler's *The Act of Creation*, to which I have previously referred in my preface. Koestler naturally takes account of the pioneer essays of Freud[3] and of Bergson[4] but he goes much beyond them. He explains convincingly that a comic effect is the product of a sudden bisociation of an idea or event with two habitually incompatible frames of reference or associative contexts.[5] If this sounds a little abstruse, then the applicaion of it will perhaps make it easier to understand. For this purpose I have chosen, in the first instance, one of the humorous remarks attributed to Jesus in Matthew 23.23f.

> Woe to you, scribes and Pharisees, hypocrites! for you tithe mint and dill and cummin, and have neglected the weightier matters of the law, justice and mercy and faith; these you ought to have done, without neglecting the others. You blind guides, straining out a gnat and swallowing a camel!

The intention of this attack upon the Pharisees is quite clear. They are to be condemned for a concentration upon minutiae to the detriment of the more important aspects of moral behaviour. They bother to tithe insignificant plants – cummin, for example, that produces a minute seed used as a spice in bread or meat (Isa. 28.25, 27) – but neglect what is really significant, viz. justice, mercy and faith. Then humour is employed to make the point more effectively: they strain out the gnat but swallow the camel.

This is a very clear example, to use Koestler's terminology, of two independent matrices of perception or reasoning interacting with each other and producing a collision that ends in laughter. The one frame of reference relates to a minute insect, so small that, unless care is taken, it can be consumed inadvertently. The other frame of reference relates to a large animal which cannot be consumed whole – certainly not without noticing it – and is more often thought of as a beast of burden than a form of nourishment. Swallowing is the focal concept or link between the two mental planes and it is this that produces the bisociation, i.e. while the purpose of the filtering is to prevent swallowing something very small, it is pursued with such misplaced concern that the person in question is unaware that something huge, viz. a camel, humps and all, is gliding down past his Adam's apple.

Jesus thus accepts the premiss of the Pharisee that one should avoid consuming a gnat which has every chance of being unclean, e.g. by simply brushing the clothes of a Gentile, but he accepts it in order to expose its implicit absurdity. Hence Jesus is using irony and enters into the spirit of the other's game in order to demonstrate that its rules are stupid. This nonsense humour is all the more effective because Jesus pretends that what he says makes sense – whereas in fact it is quite impossible to swallow a camel whole. His humour therefore reveals itself by bringing together two statements – one of which is palpably false – and telescoping them into a single line that gives the impression of being a popular adage or proverb. There is a bisociation which displaces attention from the gnat to the camel.

One other example, from an extra-biblical source, will be sufficient to make this kind of analysis clear.

> CAR DEALER: You get into this car at midnight and at 4 a.m. you are in Grimsby.
>
> INDIGNANT CUSTOMER: And what am I to do in Grimsby in the middle of the night?

The customer's question is perfectly logical but it has no bearing on the subject under discussion, which is the speed of the car. The link-concept is 'Grimsby at 4 a.m.' – which in one frame of reference serves as a chance example, while in the other it has an essential part. This sudden shift to a seemingly irrelevant aspect of a bisociated concept is that which marks humour and produces laughter.[6]

It is precisely because Niebuhr did not penetrate far enough in his understanding of humour that he was led to expel it from the sanctuary. For him humour is concerned with incongruities, between the false dignity of the proud man slipping on the banana skin and his undignified acrobatics as he vainly tries to preserve his balance. But Niebuhr did not see that we are here dealing with two separate matrices. In terms of this hackneyed example, there is the hubris of mind contrasted with the earthly materiality of the body, or it may be said that laughter arises at the line of intersection between one plane of exaltation and the other of trivialization. Failure to think through the nature of the 'incongruity' – to use his term – that he found at the basis of the comic also led Niebuhr to contrast it with the life of faith. He saw a discrepancy between the goodness of God and the evil we encounter in the world, between the vastness of the universe and the apparent insignificance of human beings and their thirst for infinity, between suffering on the one hand and the divine love and mercy on the other. These do not fit, according to him, into 'any neat picture of the whole', and they can only be resolved by faith and not by humour. A preliminary comment on my part might be that maybe they will never be resolved by faith, while perhaps humour will enable us to live with them. However these incongruities, over which Niebuhr agonized, belong to a single frame of reference – God's world – they do not arise, as does laughter, out of different matrices. In other words the incongruities that appalled Niebuhr all lie within one frame, while the 'incongruities' from which laughter stems involve two independent matrices. Not understanding humour sufficiently Niebuhr did not grasp the essential character of laughter and too readily switched from it to the complexities of understanding the meaning of life. So he ended up by opposing the immediate incongruities of living, with which he believed laughter to be concerned, to the ultimate ones – sin, death, etc. – which are faith's preoccupation in his eyes. This contrast was falsely based because the 'incongruities' are not of the same kind. The argument is then a *non sequitur* and does not establish the incompatibility of laughter and faith.

In true comic manner, but quite unconsciously, Niebuhr made two further mistakes, in that he assumed that the ultimate and the penultimate and that worship and everyday life do not belong to the same frame of reference. But in fact there is no necessary disjunction between them. The way towards the ultimate is through the penultimate, i.e. through the common or garden stuff of our daily lives, which is the subject matter both of comedy and of tragedy and the context within which we have to exercise faith. To assume that when we enter a church building all that is contingent is left behind, that from there we can exclude the incongruities of life and that faith can focus itself entirely upon the ultimate is to be misled as to the nature of Christian worship.

Worship itself uses the penultimate as a way to the ultimate. It takes bread and wine – earthly penultimate realities – as vehicles of union with Christ – the ultimate. When we cross the church threshold, we do not enter eternity. Rather worship is an activity that springs out of life in the world; it is a celebration – a high point – of that life and is based upon world-involvement and not upon world-rejection. It is an encounter with the holy and makes explicit the union of the ultimate with the penultimate, of the sacred with the secular, by showing that the holy is a dimension of the whole of life. Worship opens up the secular to the holy and assists us to find the holy in everyday life. Worship celebrates hope, brings the hoped-for future into contact with the present and provides a stimulus for reshaping the world into a more human place.[7] If humour and laughter are based upon the penultimate, so is worship. If worship is grounded in the reality of human existence before God, so is laughter. There need be no incompatibility between them.

Nor can laughter just be dismissed from the cultus as if it belonged to the sphere of the profane while worship is some all-holy and set apart activity. I have argued elsewhere at length, and need not repeat the several points in detail here, that through Christ the division between the sacred and the profane has been overcome,[8] and that 'profane' is a category which is foreign to the New Testament as a whole and is ultimately meaningless for Christians. In and through the incarnation the holy has come down to the level of the profane so that what is common may be elevated to the level of the holy. Even the very phraseology used by Niebuhr – holy of holies – is rooted in the Old Testament and not in the New – it refers to the temple at Jerusalem and not to Christian churches. Indeed the buildings where Christians gather for worship, from the dining rooms of private houses to the great cathedrals of later days, are not so many Jerusalem temples nor are they numinous areas belonging to a sphere separate from the world of human endeavour.[8] Laughter then is no more inappropriate in a church than in a dining room.

Of course every Christian is called to be a person of faith, but this does not mean that all questions are answered, all incongruities removed, all doubts set at rest. Indeed doubt is the corollary of faith and a faith that is never questioned is far from mature. As Bultmann has expressed it: 'when I venture *in* faith, I also venture *faith itself*.'[10] We do not then leave our doubts outside the church building when we enter to worship. We are not so preoccupied with the ultimate that our concern with the incongruities of the world – in Niebuhr's sense – can be simply discarded or temporarily quieted. Indeed, in some respects, Niebuhr seems to have been speaking out of a pre-Christian context. He affirmed that laughter cannot deal with the problem of sin and that we do not laugh in our prayers because it is a solemn experience to be judged by God. Yet no one supposes that laughter can cleanse from sin, but most Christians believe that Christ himself has dealt with it on the cross, and that they have received the forgiveness of sins through baptism when they died to sin in order no longer to be its slaves (Rom. 6.1–14). Christians come together as the redeemed, the liberated, as those who have been justified by faith. Granted that they are *justi et peccatores* – justified but still sinners – not every prayer brings them under judgment. What of praise, thanksgiving and joy before the Lord? Cannot this joy express itself in laughter? Is it not fitting that the eucharist as a joyful feast should be accompanied by some degree of merriment?

Here we must acknowledge the distinction between laughter *with* and laughter *at*. The former is most frequently associated in the Bible with joy. So in the Lucan form of the beatitudes we read: 'Blessed are you that weep now, for you shall laugh' (6.21b), i.e. those who are miserable shall laugh in the joy of sharing in the blessings that God has in store for them. Then they will be able to sing with the psalmist:

> Our mouth was filled with laughter
> and our tongue with shouts of joy (Ps.126.2).

The same imagery is used in the book of Job by Bildad the Shuhite looking forward to the day when God

> will yet fill your mouth with laughter,
> and your lips with shouting (Job 8.21).

Can one persist in maintaining that the laughter that God gives is somehow out of place in the worship of the same God?

Laughter *at* from the biblical perspective is a way of deriding evil. It expresses scorn and hence 'the Lord laughs at the wicked' (Ps. 37.13; cf. 59.8). It is then a form of protest, a blow for freedom. For laughter to accompany a celebration of the eucharist in a situation of oppression is to transcend servitude and affirm the right to liberation. Such a perspective enables us to appreciate that the singing of a music hall song, with all its bitter humour, can take it place in a celebration of freedom. It is in fact very right and proper that in a selection of texts bearing on salvation today the Commission on World Mission and Evangelism of the WCC included this cabaret poem by Hanna Dieter Hüsch:

> I'd like to be a clown
> Never seen without a laugh
> I'd like to be a clown
> Making other people laugh.
> I'd like to be a clown calm and serene
> No impressive hero
> But a tiny little joker
> In a world of bitter pain.
>
> Instead of saying yes to everything I meet
> I'd like to turn somersaults in every city street.
> I'd like to thumb my nose on a grey and gloomy day
> At the hardened rascal who meets me in the way.
> I'd like to pull a long face when the sun begins to shine
> And give a puppet to the child who weeps at evening time.
> I should like the world to laugh a while
> Before it's too late
> I'd like to be a clown
> Whose head is already slightly cracked.
>
> I'd like to clamber over rooftops on all fours
> To see the poor poor and the rich rich
> from above, how they eat their bread and how,
> accordingly, they rate their prospects.
> I'd like them all to laugh
> and not to disgrace their neighbour.
>
> I'd like to stand on corners
> Scattering a Scherzo on the streets
> For their benefit and at my expense.
> I'd like to stand guard over a laugh

On an abandoned post.
I should like the world to laugh a while
Before it's too late.
I'd like to be a clown
Whose heart is a merry planet.[11]

Here is topsy-turvydom – the world turned upside down – saying no to the *status quo*, disclosing the possibility of a different future, of different values than those that result in poverty and pain. It is a song of protest that derides what is in order to bring what may be a little nearer. It speaks to the present in laughing terms of the future. It fits without any disease into an act of worship understood as 'a kind of celebrative kick, a jovial good natured, profoundly hilarious laughter in the presence of murky devils'.[12] There seems to be in fact a certain natural affinity between laughter and Christian worship – but let us pursue our understanding of the comic a little further.

The function of the comic, says Nathan A. Scott, is 'to be an example of the contingent, imperfect, earth bound creatures that in truth we really are, and it is also his function to awaken in us a lively recognition of what in fact our true status is.'[13] Comedy perpetually recalls to us that we are human and finite and not divine and infinite – a fact that many dictators, lacking a sense of humour, are never able to accept. Whereas comedy prevents us from forgetting our humanity with all its weaknesses and foibles. It keeps us rooted, therefore, in empirical reality. Without this earthing, as it were, in laughter, faith would issue in dogmatism, while laughter without faith leads to despair. 'The sacred needs the comic as much as the comic needs the sacred; for the comic apart from its basis in the sacred, or the sacred apart from the qualification of the comic, are equally prey to distortion.'[14] Without laughter piety becomes pride, devotion fanaticism and the sacred the demonic. Indeed humour is an important defence against absolutism. So Wolfgang M. Zucker asks: 'Is not the clown perhaps himself the laughter of the Infinite about the Finite when it pretends to be absolute?'[15] But worship needs this laughter as much as anything else.

Worship needs laughter especially in connection with two temptations to which Christians are particularly prone. The first is the absolutizing of our forms of worship and the second is the absolutizing of our images of God. When some Roman Catholics rail against the substitution of the vernacular mass for one in a long-dead language or when some Anglicans object to Series 2 or 3 in favour of an order already 400 years old, both groups are failing to realize that all forms of worship are of human devising. Granted that the structure of the eucharist – taking bread and wine, blessing God, breaking the bread and distributing the elements – may go back to Jesus at the Last Supper, nevertheless all communion services are the product of human activity.To hold that one language or text is sacrosanct is to be guilty of absolutization which humour can do much to undermine. Humour too prevents the absolutization of that which we hold most sacred – including our images of God as well as our forms of worship – and this is necessary because we can neither possess nor be as God. To think otherwise is to give way to idolatry and to that pride which laughter cannot tolerate or allow.

The logic of what I have said so far is moving in the direction of recognizing that the eucharist is a comedy and not a tragedy. Not that the tragic and comic perspectives are necessarily always incompatible, since both refer to the same human condition. Nor is it sheer callousness to detect the comic even in suffering. Amidst the horrors of the Nazi concentration camps, some of the inmates were able to laugh and to appreciate that the comic is an essential ingredient of the human condition. They perceived that in the last analysis the Nazis were ridiculous.[16] Evil after all, is not only sinful, it is stupid and can be treated comically. But Niebuhr misses this: 'There is no humour in the scene of Christ upon the cross.'[17] It is true that such laughter as there was, according to the gospels, was laugher *at* in the sense of scorn on the part of those who mocked Jesus (Mark 15.29ff.; Luke 23.35f.), but there was nonetheless the humour of irony. Those responsible for the crucifixion of Jesus were seeking to accomplish one thing, whereas in fact they achieved something else which was in accordance with the will of God. They meant to eliminate a troublemaker and they helped to inaugurate a new age! Those who perceive the reality of what was taking place cannot be blamed if their natural sorrow at the suffering of Jesus is mingled with the laughter of joy at what he was accomplishing. 'There is after all a merriment which is possible for living life even when one aspect of life is excruciating pain.'[18]

Yet there is a difference between the tragic hero and the clown. The former challenges the gods; he seeks to defy finitude. He struggles with all his might, while realizing that he cannot break out of the walls that imprison him and spell his doom. Tragedy indeed is the perception of the human situation under the aspect of immanence. The comic however calls the very walls in question – topsy-turvydom as I suggested above in relation to Hüsch's poem. The comic embodies the hope that we need not be confined eternally within that which regulates our lives. In other words, comedy is the perception of the human situation under the aspect of transcendence.[19] Consequently comedy stands more close to the Christian viewpoint than does tragedy. The Christian does not seek to challenge God nor to deny his or her own imperfections and incongruities. In this sense, the comic role, which is rooted in contingency and finitude, is the appropriate style of Christian discipleship. (Did not Francis of Assisi call his followers *joculatores*, God's merrymen?) Similarly, the eucharist is not the commemoration of a tragic hero nor a perpetual funeral memorial of a dead Jew who battled unsuccessfully against overwhelming odds. It is the recalling of one who did indeed die, but rose again and who thereby illuminated the human condition under the aspect of transcendence. The Christian spirit then at all times, including attendance at a eucharist, expresses itself not in 'a nihilistic guffaw but a redeeming smile'.[20]

The humour of which I speak is not of course to be identified with farce, which does trivialize the human situation. To treat a subject humorously is not to treat it lightly – that would rather be the effect of frivolity. Comedy in its highest form is a search for and a discovery of truth. Comedy presupposes meaning in the very act of not taking its subject matter with absolute seriousness. Only when there is recognition of the possibility of significance and of hope is true comedy present, for it does not, *pace* Niebuhr, reveal a gap in coherence. It does indeed reject facile conformity – as does the worship of a crucified and risen Lord – but its very effect depends upon an acceptance of an underlying coherence and order. It is not anarchic but defends being against the pure concept or category. Jesus himself inveighed, and used humour to do so, against the existing Pharisaic order, against those who, from Moses' seat, imposed too great a burden on the people, but he did so in the name of a more profound order. The medieval Feast of Fools was equally a protest against the non-human and this comic inversion of the liturgy began with the Magnificat and its verse: 'He has put down the mighty from their seat and has exalted the humble and meek.' This reversal of roles, with the minor orders celebrating a mock liturgy, was only comic because everyone accepted the importance of the mass and the priest's office was taken with deadly seriousness.[21] There was indeed much laughter in the medieval churches, but once the underlying security of religion had gone, e.g. with the onset of the Reformation, then laughter was excluded. Those who condemn laughter at worship speak out of human insecurity and not from faith, whereas, in the words of M. Conrad Hyers, 'in its most mature form laughter arises within the freedom of security'.[22]

We joke most frequently about that which we hold to be of central concern. It is not surprising then that Jewish comedians often laugh at Jews and that blacks are comic at the expense of their own colour and that theologians are sometimes humorous about God and the church. 'In laughter,' to quote Hyers again, 'seriousness is made human and tolerable at the same time that it is preserved from stuffiness and prudishness,' and he goes on to comment that 'holiness apart from humour is inhuman'.[23]

That laughter should be an accompaniment of worship also follows from one further consideration. Christian worship is a corporate activity; it is the celebration of a community in fellowship. We do not of course joke readily with strangers, but then Christians are members one of another. Now laughter usually functions within a communicative relation; it is part of an interactive process which constitutes social living. Laughter must be shared and so it promotes cohesion because it involves an element of reciprocity.

> To laugh, or to occasion laughter through humour and wit, is to invite those present to come close. Laughter and humour are indeed like an invitation, be it an invitation for dinner, or an invitation to start a conversation: it aims at decreasing social distance.[24]

Laughter is therefore ideally suited to an act of worship which stems from and is intended to promote fellowship – but this is one way of defining the eucharist. Moreover without laughter a eucharist loses a necessary ingredient of mature interpersonal relations. 'When the spirit of comedy has departed,' writes George Santayana, 'company becomes constraint, reserve eats up the spirit, and people fall into the penurious melancholy in their scruple to be always exact, sane and reasonable.'[25] Does any reader think that this is an accurate description of some act of worship in which he or she has joined? If so, laughter provides a possible remedy. In any case, as I intimated earlier, not to bring laughter before God is to omit an essential aspect of human nature. If worship be the offering of the total self to God, how can we forget the comic?

If it be accepted, in the light of the above, that laughter and worship are compatible and that indeed on occasion their association is right and proper, it remains to be considered how practically this can be effected. Where there are fixed liturgies, the scope for humour is obviously strictly limited. When worship is according to set forms with prescribed words, it would be absurd to include humour within the given text. A joke which is amusing the first time may be so at a second and third hearing, but when one reaches the twentieth repeat it becomes downright boring. Laughter, after all, has a certain spontaneous character that fits ill with that which is rigidly regulated in advance. This means that there are in fact only three possible places where laughter may be enjoyed in a fixed liturgy: at the sermon, in the notices and possibly in the biddings to extempore prayers if provision is made for them. However, if congregations engage in liturgical creativity, by which I mean that the members themselves devise and celebrate their own forms of worship, making use of their gifts to that end, including the gift of humour,[26]* then obviously laughter could and should find a greater place. Indeed if dancing, discussions, etc., become features of the celebrations of the eucharist, then laughter may be heard once more. Then we may come closer to what Dennis Potter, in a television review in *The Sunday Times* of 18 December 1977, has called 'the comedy, the relaxed hilarity, the sheer, bountiful, clown-like, playful zest which is so often at the heart of religious truth. It is,' he continues, 'because there is a God – or, rather, that God *is* – that I want to kick a tin-can down the street or run a stick along the railings.' It is precisely for the same reason that I want on occasion in worship to laugh before the Lord.

Let me conclude with another quotation that, in fact, reverses that with which I began this chapter but which I believe this chapter fully validates:

> Even in the holy of holies men are *set free* by the ultimate presence of God, so that in that fellowship they can offer whatever gifts they come bearing, including the gift of humour.[27]

EPILOGUE

Participation and Creativity

The method which I adopted for this book and which I specified
in my preface has involved the association of worship and other
subjects with which it is not usually related. Because of this
deliberate divergence the preceding chapters could be read as so
many self-contained and independent essays. In fact, as I pointed
out initially, the topics have not been arbitrarily selected and they
are related as so many links in a logical chain. There are in addition
a number of recurring themes that serve to unite the sections. I am
not referring simply to the fact that each one is concerned with
worship and that this therefore constitutes a central subject that
binds everything together: I have in mind some specific topics that
I wish to call attention to and two in particular that I propose to
elaborate in this Epilogue. The major recurring items are: the
celebrative character of the eucharist together with the ideas of
newness, change, identity, salvation, freedom, risk, participation
and creativity.

Christian worship is essentially a feast of celebration. A church
building is a house of celebration; the arts that contribute to the
setting of worship have a celebrative character and the eucharist
itself celebrates Christ's victory in his conflict with evil and death.
It is then an occasion of joy of which dancing is an appropriate and
indeed natural expression. This gladness also arises from the
recognition of future possibilities and the experience of what is new.
As a game, its outcome is not foreclosed and so it breaks the bonds
of the *status quo*. As story time, it tells of God's future. Indeed it is
a celebration and foretaste of that future, and hence in speaking of
dance, conflict and politics I have referred to the eucharist as an
anticipation of the messianic banquet. Again – still in terms of
newness and the future – the eucharist, I have suggested, is a
political act that reveals the *eschaton* as the direction for the implementation of justice and it is consequently a feast of hope. The

worshipping community then constitutes itself as a sign of the future of society, and from time to time its members laugh at what is, in order to bring a little nearer what may be.

Worship is consequently very much bound up with change, since to anticipate and in part to bring in the new necessitates transformation. Hence the importance of conflict which assists adaption to new conditions, unfreezes archaic attitudes and facilitates the acceptance of new perspectives that can be temporarily 'refrozen' through worship. Then worship is also a summons to rebellion, to join Christ in his continuing battle on behalf of the Kingdom of God.

Granted that continual change can produce an identity crisis – for identity requires some element of continuity – then worship as a game with rules provides some regularity that can help avoid this danger. Our identity as followers of Jesus is also fostered through our playing of the Last Supper and identifying with him, and if we also join in a eucharistic dance then we may be on the way to identifying with our bodies. Further the legitimate conflicts in which we have to engage as Jesus' disciples promote our cohesion as his community.

Yet another theme that runs through every chapter is that of salvation and only a few indications are needed to stress its centrality. So we have noted that salvation is equivalent to wholeness, which is achieved in part by the use of our potentialities as in full play, in part by the unification of the spiritual and physical through dance. Salvation too has been understood as coming to terms with our sexuality, while conflict has been interpreted as setting free both the oppressed and oppressors from a dehumanizing situation so that both may approach more nearly to wholeness, which has therefore a political dimension.

All this relates at practically every turn to freedom. One cannot enjoy worship as a game unless it is liberated from entire domination by rules and unvariable fixed scenarios so that we can be players ourselves and not puppets. Yet we need some rules to ensure a framework for freedom. If worship is a game of liberation, then through dance we may seek the liberation of the body. As a fellowship we must be free to relate and so we must be able to conflict, while appreciating that conflict itself may promote freedom. Must we not be free to laugh so that laughter can express our liberation? Must not worship itself be liberating if it is to mean anything to us and to the world at large, opening the present to the future and pointing to political models of freedom?

Of course all these ways of thinking about and doing worship carry risks. Freedom has its casualties; sexuality can be explosive; conflict may be harmful; political debate may reveal deep and unsuspected divisions. Yet must not all these possibilities be faced if worship is to be an adventure and an exploration, instead of a haven of security from which life has ebbed away?

I come now to the last two of my catalogue of recurring themes, viz. to participation and to creativity, to which I want to devote much more space than to the other items because I consider that the understanding of these is fundamental to our whole concept and practice of worship. Before launching into an analysis, let me recall some of the principal points at which the first of these – participation – emerged in the preceding chapters. In terms of play, worship, which is social play and not so many games of solitaire, requires interaction; it is a group game that can be an exploration of the possibilities of relationship. In terms of dance, I have spoken of communal rejoicing and this is only real when all take an active part. Sexuality, conflict, politics, humour – all refer to interaction and so to participation. However, enough of these generalities: let us consider participation more directly.

Both in terms of its etymology (*participationem/particeps*) and of usage in the past, participation means essentially the action or fact of partaking, i.e. of taking a part in or sharing. So it is customary to speak of partaking a meal, but this very example emphasizes the extent to which participation is something that is active. To partake of a meal does involve eating. Passivity is thus the negation of participation. If I say that I did not participate in a certain conversation, this means that I said nothing, although I might well have been present. As applied to a play, only those who are cast as the characters in the comedy or tragedy can be said to have a part and so to be participators. In this properly active sense no member of an audience can be said to participate in a play. If any one were to do so, he or she would cease to be a member of the audience – which basically means a group of hearers (*audientes*) – and would be playing a part in the drama itself.

This distinction between the performers of the central action and those who only see or hear what others are doing is preserved in everyday speech. If I were to announce that I had taken part in a singing competition, it would be understood that I had been one of the singers or at least an accompanist or a judge, not that I just sat in the hall and listened to the competitors. Again one can speak of taking part in a concert if one is a musician, otherwise we *go* to a concert. If I take part in *a* play, then I take a part in a play – it may be a leading or a minor part but in either case it will involve my acting. Yet if I sit in an audience I cannot be said to be participating, however much I appreciate and enjoy the scenes unfolding before me.

Consequently to speak of audience participation is really to blur the distinction between onlookers and performers. Attempts to promote audience participation are so many efforts to involve the audience directly in the action so that they cease to be passive – cease indeed to be audience and become performers. Hence at the climax of the musical 'Godspell', members of the audience were invited on to the stage to partake of some wine with the players; as soon as they did, they ceased to be audience and became actors. An actor after all is one who acts, i.e. is active, I am not saying that there is anything reprehensible in such a proceeding. It was indeed a fitting climax to a moving production. I am simply pointing out that to describe this as audience participation when it is a process whereby an audience ceases to be an audience – if only momenttarily – is to be guilty of an imprecise use of terms.

Sometimes clear and obvious distinctions are obscured when, for example, someone declares that he or she participated in a concert by reading the score. This is not to take part in the normal sense of the word. The person in view has not played a part in the making of the music which is the primary activity making a concern what it is and not the meeting of a literary society. The form that participation takes will differ, of course, depending upon the activity being undertaken in common. A debate requires speaking; a dance demands physical movement; an attack upon a military objective involves the use of weapons; a game of tennis is not possible without the wielding of rackets and the hitting of balls – and so on. But the occupants of the visitors' gallery in the House of Commons do not take part in the debate; the spectators at a ballet do not themselves dance; a television crew filming the onslaught on a bridge are not participators in a military advance; the crowd around the centre court at Wimbledon are just not playing tennis.

Yet the distinction between active and passive is not absolute.

My appreciation of a symphony may certainly be increased by my careful following of a score; my enjoyment of a discussion will depend upon my following the argument in my mind. In both these instances I am not entirely passive, but nevertheless clarity is obscured if one speaks of participation in these situations. Again my presence at a tragedy may lead to catharsis or I may identify with one or other of the characters and so become involved in those ways, but I would suggest that to call this participation is not really accurate. Unless we observe the difference in meaning between words we shall lose clarity of thought. I do not want to stress that participation has a particular meaning in order to uphold some preconceived ideas about worship or about any other human activity; I simply want to use participation in a precise manner so that we all know and agree what we are talking about when the term is employed. Audience *reaction*, for example, is a right and proper subject for analysis, but investigation will not be helped by interpreting it as participation. It is perfectly possible to act a play with no audience at all and no possibility therefore of audience reaction, but one cannot have a performance without some persons to play the various parts. On the other hand audience reaction can be shared. I can join in the applause which is a response to a beautifully sung aria or a finely delineated character. I may share in laughter at some uproarious farce, provided only that I laugh myself. This is part of audience reaction to a performance, but it is not part of the performance itself, even though there may be a certain interaction between performers and audience, in that the former may be stimulated to greater efforts by the reaction of the latter.

Participation is of course impossible apart from others. When an individual can achieve an objective on his own, he does not think of participation. So if I light a cigarette with a match from a box I possess, I am in no way participating, sharing, in anything. But if I haven't a match and someone else strikes one of his own for me, he is participating in the lighting of my cigarette. Participation, therefore, refers to a collective action, in which of course an individual has a part to play, but it does involve interaction between people.[1] It requires one to enter into a relationship. Since to partake means sharing in, then it is with other people that we share. Since it also means to take a part, the other parts have to be played by other people. To recognize this is again to stress the active side of participation and at the same time to draw attention to its outward-looking aspect. Six people sitting silently in a room may all be meditating upon the same subject; but there can be no question of participation (unless telepathy is both a fact and is intensely operative upon the given occasion). It is only when thoughts are shared, i.e. when the six express themselves and address one another, that participation becomes a reality. If the six remain speechless, it is absurd to say that they are participating in an act of meditation. There are in fact six separate acts of meditation going on and they could just as well go on in six separate rooms. It is when there is a sharing of ideas, aspirations, etc., that it is accurate to speak of participation in an act of meditation.

Participation thus involves my taking part in a joint activity. If however I take more than my part and usurp that of someones else, I am blocking his or her participation. In other words, participation does not mean that I have to do *everything*, because then its primary reference to sharing is denied. Conversely if I do nothing at all I cannot share in what is taking place.

So far I have been making some general observations about participation and illustrating them in particular from concert and theatre going. It is now time to apply them to worship. It seems to me obvious, in view of what has been said above and in the preceding chapters, that to speak of participation in worship is to refer to an activity in which one engages oneself as distinct from the more or less passive observance of something done by someone else. So the early Christians, to use the image of a drama, were actors in their worship and not members of an audience, or, if one thinks of worship as a game, they were players and not spectators. Many of today's worshippers appear to attend on the understanding that they are detached, but that is not to worship. In other words, when the priests in the Middle Ages changed from doing something 'on behalf of' the congregation to doing something 'instead of' the congregation, the congregation had virtually ceased to participate in worship. Consequently one should reject as a norm for Christian worship today anything based upon a comparison between priests and actors on the one hand and between congregation and audience on the other. In Christian worship all are to be performers, although each one or each group may have different parts to play. This means that to participate in worship is to contribute to what is taking place and to enter into relationships with one's fellow worshippers. There should clearly be variety in the kinds of contributions; these will depend upon the gifts we bring and develop through use. This, as we have seen, was recognized by Paul (Principle v, above p. 7) who told the Corinthians: 'When you come together, each one has a hymn, a lesson, a revelation, a tongue, or an interpretation' (I Cor. 14.26). It was appreciated by the author to the Ephesians in terms of reciprocity when he wrote: 'Be filled with the Spirit, addressing one another in psalms and hymns and spiritual songs, singing and making melody to the Lord with all your heart' (Eph. 5.18f.).

At the same time – let me repeat – such participation does not require any one individual seeking to do everything. He or she should have *a* part to play, leaving the others to fulfil their parts. Thus we do not have to say every prayer ourselves; if we hear a prayer uttered by someone else, we may join in (participate) and make it our own by saying Amen, because in this way, as Justin Martyr said centuries ago, we 'express our assent'.[2]

Yet while we do not have to do everything, there are degrees of participation that have to be safeguarded. Always to express assent to someone else's formula and never to speak oneself is scarcely to be active. Indeed while in a play not everyone can have the major roles and some have to act minor characters, if the same people always have the important parts and the same group the less important ones some frustration on the part of the latter will inevitably make itself evident. Similarly if there is not give and take in Christian worship, if leading roles are not shared out, those who are always required to play second fiddle will feel that the degree of participation allowed them is insufficient to make the act of worship *their* worship. Instead of worship helping them to expand and advance towards liberation they will be inhibited and repressed.

What then – to apply these observations by way of illustration to a particular example – what about 'participation' in a cathedral evensong? There are two ways of approaching this question, one of which I would contend is false. The incorrect procedure would be to start by accepting without question that what takes place at a cathedral evensong is worship – on such grounds as that there are clergy involved, prayers are offered and psalms are sung. The next step is to acknowledge that worship requires participation and then to affirm that since cathedral evensong is an act of worship participation must be taking place! The circular and therefore unhelpful nature of this argument will be obvious. In contrast to this, the correct procedure, I would hold, starts from a precise definition of participation, as given above, and this then leads logically to the observation that the degree of participation possible for a congregation in a cathedral can only be very limited. The music will be the almost exclusive province of the organist and choir, while the prayers will be read or intoned by one of the cathedral staff. The congregation may utter the occasional Amen – though frequently Amens are sung to very elaborate settings – but there will be little relationship between those present and in general they will be more akin to an audience at a performance than to a gathering of Christians to worship God. There will in fact be interactive deficiency which either prevents the recognition of identity or results in identity deprivation[3] so that any apprehension of the corporate nature of Christian worship will be difficult if not impossible. Nor will there be much interchange of major roles from week to week. The same highly trained and skilled personnel will be to the fore at each service. Now obviously there is no reason why there should not be attempts to offer to God the most perfect musical renderings of praise that are humanly possible, but as a staple diet, as a regular form of Christian *corporate* worship, it must be regarded as questionable precisely because it does not permit enough in the way of participation to enable one to say that one has a real (as distinct from a token) part or share in the proceedings. Moreover such participation as is possible seems to be envisaged largely in verbal and cerebral terms and I have been at pains throughout this book to stress that this is simply not adequate, although our inheritance from the Reformation has predisposed us to think otherwise. It has led us to understand participation largely in terms of literacy and understanding. Let me explain what I mean.

Where there is a fixed order of service and a printed version is available, obviously participation can take the form of reading together and aloud certain of the prescribed prayers. But this form of participation may be limited in two ways: first, it does not apply to those who cannot read and, second, even if people can read they will be unable to do so if there are insufficient copies of the service to go round. Although these remarks may seem a little obvious, they do have a direct bearing on the subject of participation at the time of the Reformation which needs to be examined since it influences us still today although largely unconsciously. Ignorance of the facts might lead one to suppose that the publication of services in the vernacular was a definite move towards a more congregational type of worship as contrasted with the priest-ridden medieval practice. In one sense it was, but only in the sense that the laity were now able to *follow* what the priest said with some understanding. Hence in the preface to the 1549 *Book of Common Prayer* – a typical example of a certain Reformation viewpoint – the principal objection to the previous use of Latin is stated as follows:

> Whereas S. Paul would have such language spoken to the people in the church, as they might understand and have profit by hearing the same; the service in this Church of England (these many years) hath been read in Latin to the people, which they understood not; so that they have heard with their ears only; and their hearts, spirit, and mind, have not been edified thereby.

Consistent with this – 'language spoken *to* the people . . . the service hath been read *to* the people' – the new communion service of 1549 in English allotted practically nothing to the laity. When anyone other than the priest has anything to say or sing, it is specified that this shall be 'the Clerkes'. Hence the *Gloria in excelsis*, the Creed, the *Sanctus* and the *Agnus Dei* are all assigned to them. Even the General Confession is to be said 'in the name of all that are minded to receive the holy Communion, either by one of them, or else by one of the ministers, or by the priest himself'. Similarly the Prayer of Humble Access is to be said by the priest 'in the name of all them that shall receive the Communion' (1549, 1552, 1662). In the case of the Confession, where one of the intending communicants is specified, literacy may well be a cause of the restriction, whereby the people do not confess their own sins but someone else does it for them – but is this participation? However let us look a little more closely at the subject of literacy.

One of the effects of the Renaissance was a great stress upon the importance of learning; it is this that explains the foundation of so large a number of schools in the century from 1550 to 1650, and the consequent increase in literacy.[4] However whereas in 1533 Sir Thomas More made a somewhat ambiguous statement that suggests that he thought there was a literacy rate in England of about 50%, fourteen years later Stephen Gardiner, Bishop of Worcester, remarked that 'not the hundredth part of the realm' could read.[5] It has been suggested that in Shakespearian London between a third and half of the people were literate, but it must not be forgotten that the majority of the population lived in the countryside where the number of those who could read was probably much smaller. This rural illiteracy was due partly to lack of schools but also to the conditions of agricultural life for which reading was by no means essential. Indeed even those who did learn their letters often lost the ability to use their knowledge because they possessed no books and spent their time at the plough or spinning wheel.[6]

Apart from the question of literacy limiting the possibility of participation by reading, there is also the matter of the number of copies available and this in part was affected by the cost. Of the 1549 book at least four editions were published before Whitsunday of that year, two of them early in March and two of them in May, and in some instances there could have been more than one impression of the same edition.[7] Nevertheless there never was any likelihood that copies would be available for each and every worshipper, nor was the need recognized – after all, services are to be read '*to* the people' and not *by* the people. In addition to the questions of reading ability and availability of copies, the cost of each one was such that only well off individuals could afford their own, while parish churches were not in a position to purchase great quantities.

Those prayer books on sale on 7 March cost two shillings in paperback and three shillings and four pence in hard covers. By June these prices had risen to two shillings and two pence and four shillings respectively,[8] while the Elizabethan book cost the church of Yatton in Somerset five shillings when it came out in 1559[9] and the church of St Michael, Cornhill, laid out five shillings and one penny 'for the New Order of the Service Book' on 27 February 1560.[10] Since an ordinary clergyman earned between ten to twenty pounds a year, then to buy a *Book of Common Prayer* with hard covers in June 1549 would cost a thirtieth of his stipend, if he was at the minimum, i.e. twelve days' pay, while if he were at twenty pounds he would have to spend nearly a week's salary. It is not surprising that the churchwardens' accounts indicate that few churches had more than one copy.[11]

It we take the literacy rate, the cost and the limited number of books to hand, we can begin to understand the tenor of certain rubrics which otherwise would be difficult to appreciate. Thus the General Confession, added to Morning Prayer in 1552, is directed to be said 'after the minister' – this was continued in 1662. Also in 1552 and 1662 the Lord's Prayer after communion is to be said by the priest 'the people repeating after him every petition'. The didactic note of these instructions is made very apparent in the marriage service which in 1549 and subsequently required the man to make the affirmation about the ring 'taught by the priest'. Moreover the deliberate abandonment of the previous custom of saying silent or secret prayers is another indication of the same didactic motive. So, for example, the eucharistic prayer of 1549 is to be said or sung 'plainly and distinctly' and the Lord's Prayer in the 1552 Morning Prayer is to be rendered 'with a loud voice'.

We are now, after this brief review, in a position to make some observations about the relationship between participation and literacy. At the time of the Reformation, participation was seen exclusively in terms of hearing and understanding. The service was to be said, read or sung *to* the people for their edification. This however is not solely a question of literacy; it is also the outcome of a certain theological stance. The extreme Protestant view about the eucharist was that it is basically a pious remembering of what Christ has accomplished – the action is then purely mental. What is required is that the people should understand in order that they may be stimulated to devout recollection.[12] Gregory Dix was certainly accurate when he asserted that

> as a strictly mental 'action' (if that be a permissible term) it has of course ceased to be anything at all of a 'corporate' action. . . . From being the action that creates the unity of the Church as the Body of Christ, the eucharist has become precisely that which *breaks down the Church into separate individuals*.[13]

At the present day however, when most people who attend a service in the West are literate, it is possible to see this literacy as enabling one form of participation denied to our sixteenth-century predecessors. It is now possible for the prayers to be said or sung together by all so that participation is not just following in the mind but actually a voicing of the prayers. It is an acceptance of this fact – consciously or not – that explains the large number of prayers allotted to 'all' in, for example, 'An Order for Holy Communion, Series Three'. Now the Collect for Purity, the *Gloria*, the Creed, the Confession, the Prayer of Humble Access, the Lord's Prayer, together with a postcommunion thanksgiving and many responses, are each and every one to be said by all together. However it has to be borne in mind that where the eucharist is celebrated in a non-literary culture this form of participation will be difficult to achieve, as it was in England at the time of the Reformation.

Despite the benefit of literacy in this respect, I must emphasize that this form of participation is not to be regarded as the only proper one. Indeed it is essentially cerebral and therefore obscures the fact that human beings are psycho-physical entities. Because they are such and because worship requires the offering of the whole self to God, there has to be the possibility of participation through the body as a whole, not just through brain and tongue. To say this is not to assume an anti-intellectual stance – to offer the entire self is to include the intellect in the offering, but to offer only the intellect through verbalization and understanding is to offer only part of oneself. It is indeed to fail to celebrate worship as a creative occasion. With this remark we pass from an analysis of participation to the second of the pair of topics I wish to elaborate in this Epilogue, viz. to creativity.

Here I am concerned not with the nature of creative thinking, as heretofore, but with the relationship between creativity *per se* and the Christian cultus. What part can or should creativity play within the actual act of worship itself? Can it in fact be an integral element, or must it always be related only in terms of the setting? That it is necessarily only connected with the background to worship may seem to be suggested by talk about the musical 'setting' of the psalms or of the creed. There seems to be here a distinction between psalms as part of worship and the tunes to which we may sing them – tunes that may therefore be dispensed with and the speaking voice only employed. However many a chorister and many an organist would assert that it is possible to worship through music and that even music without words can be an offering to God. When the composer, the instrumentalist or a soloist use their talents in a creative way are they not glorifying the Creator?

Moreover the underlying assumption that music simply enhances or intensifies the words employed in worship is a false one. Worship as I have just insisted, does not consist solely of verbalization, otherwise it becomes entirely mental and does not engage our total being which is more than the life of the mind. All the arts, music included, are so many non-verbal languages in themselves; they too communicate; they too can be celebrative. So, for example, it was said of Claud Monet that every single painting of his expressed his love of life. How many of Bach's fugues breath an air of pure devotion! Dance, I have argued, is yet another art form that does not use words but is a very fitting vehicle for worship.

The arts are, or can be, affirmations of faith, as they were in the Romanesque and Gothic eras; they can mediate a presence and so have a place in the action of worship. It is not difficult to conceive too of an artist painting a picture or drawing in the course of a service, using his creative capacity as part of worship itself, just as a musician may play and a singer may sing. In this sense the arts are not simply optional extras – pleasant adornments, as long as we can afford them – they belong to the totality of life, which includes the physical as well as the spiritual, the material as well as the mental, and it is this totality that we celebrate before the Creator and they are or should be part of that celebration.

So far when speaking of art I have been referring to the *fruits* of creativity, rather than directly to creativity itself; we must now look more closely at the meaning of that activity. To consider this is to take up a theme that most people would readily accept as valid, viz. that to produce a work of art is to be creative; but it also links up with an illuminating observation made by Dorothy L. Sayers: 'the idea of art as *creation* is, I believe, the one important contribution that Christianity has made to aesthetics.'[14]

Creation, in the sense intended here, involves the bringing into existence of something new. So Nicholas Berdyaev could assert that 'creativeness means in the first instance *imagining* something different, better and higher'.[15] Art then may include a critique of life in that it may constitute a protest against the world as it is in favour of some future model. So Hieronymus Bosch presented a devastating vision of human folly, while Picasso in his 'Guernica' thundered against the evil of human destructiveness. In contrast, it can be said that lack of creativeness leads to a concentration upon the usual or customary. The non-creative person shies away from the risk and uncertainty of the unknown and seeks the safety and security of the known. The artist, however, has the ability to produce new forms, to chance joining together elements that are usually deemed to be unrelated; he is able to free himself from the accepted norms and diverge from the habitual. Since what is produced is new, it elicits surprise. This surprise is not primarily because the object is bizarre – that would be to confuse newness with novelty, which soon palls.[16]* Rather the surprise arises from a certain quality of obviousness or perhaps better, fitness which results in a shock of recognition.[17] There is a sense of familiarity, so that, for example, when reading or hearing a poem we encounter something we did not know previously, but now that the poem has revealed it to us, we realize that, somehow or other, we have always known it. This recurring experience is sometimes termed the Eureka feeling, i.e. it prompts the reaction: This is it! I have found it – despite the fact that it is new: new not in time (Greek *neos*) but in quality (*kainos*).

Two examples should be sufficient to illustrate this intimate association between creativity and newness. The first is from the realm of literature and from a lecture on writing by Stephen Spender summarized in his autobiography.

> I pointed out that nature and people are everywhere seen at all times and places by everyone for the first time: and that the good writer is the person who retains in his work this sense of a unique moment of insight into reality. Literature, I went on, releases us from the routine of habit, reminds us of the ever-fresh experience of living, and puts us into a living relation with the past.[18]

Here literature is understood as a medium for introducing us to the ever-fresh, to the newness revealed by the creative novelist or poet.

The second illustration can be more briefly specified. One of the functions of a painter or one of the byproducts of his activity is to excite a sense of the beauty of even the most common of things, and this he achieves by seeing it afresh and lifting it into the sphere of new perception.[18] No one can ever look again at a kitchen chair in quite the same way as of old if he has once beheld the pent-up energy in Van Gogh's painting.

It is also to be affirmed that creativity, which brings what is new into being, derives from liberty. 'The mystery of creativeness,' to quote Berdyaev again, 'is the mystery of freedom.'[20] The truth of this can readily be acknowledged when one looks at what happens to the arts in a situation of unfreedom. Under the Nazis the officially accepted German paintings reached an all time low. In the USSR those contemporary works of art are of considerable merit that are exhibited out of doors and not in the galleries, and those novels that circulate underground in typescript leave the products of the orthodox Marxist writers far behind. It is also precisely because the reverse is true, viz. that 'creativeness is the way of liberation'[21] that any totalitarian regime suspects the artists and seeks to prevent the appreciation of their works by the populace at large.

But what has this to do with Christianity? The connection has already been hinted at in the previous quotation from Dorothy L. Sayers, but in any case it is doubtful if any Christian will have read this far without recalling that the first article of both the Apostles' and Nicene Creeds contains the affirmation that God is 'the Maker (or Creator) of heaven and earth'. Creativity is then an attribute or rather activity of God who, using the terms of the analysis so far, brought forth that which is new and did so freely, out of his own freedom, and indeed as an act of love. But this same God is said to have created 'man in his own image, in the image of God he created him' (Gen. 1.27). Consequently when human beings are creative, they are most like their Creator; when we create, we most nearly conform to the divine image and become co-creators with God. When we engage in creative action, we become like God. To be Godlike, i.e. to live according to his image, is to be creative. Using psychological terms, Carl F. Rogers contends that the mainspring of creativity is the human tendency to actualize ourselves, to become our potentialities.[22] This is another way of unpacking the meaning of what it is to be conformed to the divine image and so becoming creative, i.e. it is self-actualization through the use of one's gifts – creativity is both the means and the end.

In the light of this it is easy to understand why the church should look with favour on the arts and indeed actively promote them, simply because they are so many means whereby we become renewed in the image of our Creator. 'Creativeness' – this is Berdyaev once more – 'and a creative attitude to life as a whole is not man's gift, it is his duty.'[23] So it is not surprising to find William Blake, who called himself 'a Soldier of Christ',[24] affirming that 'Christianity is Art[25] . . . I know of no other Christianity and no other Gospel than the liberty both of body & mind to exercise the Divine Arts of Imagination[26] . . . Prayer is the Study of Art. Praise is the Practice of Art. Fasting &c., all relate to Art . . . indeed Jesus & his Apostles & Disciples were all Artists[27] . . . so that the Mocker of Art is the Mocker of Jesus'.[28]

However it must not be assumed that creativity refers only to those who have aesthetic talents, although this has hitherto been our main concern since we were concentrating on the arts. It is now time to recognize that there can be creativity in areas other than the arts, in science for example and also in ethics. Hence Berdyaev declares that creativeness is 'a moral imperative that applies in

every department of life'.[29] The essential correctness of this view
can easily be illustrated. So Carl F. Rogers, speaking of psycho-
therapy, observes that 'the intimate knowledge of the way in which
the individual remoulds himself in the therapeutic relationship,
with originality and effective skill, gives one confidence in the
creative potential of all individuals'.[30] While E. P. Torrance
remarks that 'there is little question but that the stifling of creativity cuts at the very root of satisfaction in living and ultimately
creates overwhelming tension and breakdown. There is also very
little doubt that man's creativity is his most valuable resource in
coping with life's daily stresses.'[31] In a word, creativity relates to
human wholeness.

Precisely because creativity is related to life in its entirety, it is
applicable to a moral response to life's situations. So there is a
distinction to be observed between an ethic of creativeness, which
is or should be that of the free person, and an ethic of law which is
appropriate to the enslaved. The Christian moral stance is not
legalistic, rather it is motivated by and directed towards love and
'the reality of love is the source of creativity'.[32] Hence ethical
behaviour, understood as being-for-others, and creativity, which
stems from love, are intimately connected. So moral consciousness
should be at all times creative and therefore inventive. The artist
can help the one not gifted in the same way, not by providing
substitute moral judgments, but by demonstrating the exercise of
freedom and by saying in effect: 'You must learn to handle practical situations as I handle the material of my book (or play or
painting): you must take them and use them to make a new thing.'[33]
Hence A. D. Lindsay could affirm that 'gracious conduct is somewhat like the work of an artist. It needs imagination and spontaneity. It is not a choice between prescribed alternatives but the
creation of something new.'[34] This last phrase brings us back to
where we started, to the newness that is a fundamental aspect of
creativity. However we must now turn to a further question, not
what has this to do with Christianity, but what has this to do with
Christian worship? In seeking to answer this I shall now relate
directly the main aspects of creativity spelt out so far to the
eucharist.

First then there is the newness that creativity brings into being.
Now 'newness' is a constant theme throughout the New Testament. Thus we read of Christ's *new* teaching (Mark 1.27), his *new*

commandment (John 13.34), the *new* covenant (I Cor. 11.25), the *new* name of Christians (Rev. 2.17), the *new* Jerusalem (Rev.3.12) and of the *new* hymn sung before the throne of God (Rev. 5.9). This is to interpret the work of Christ and its effects as re-creation or new creation: 'if any one is in Christ, he is a new creation' (II Cor. 5.17) – 'Behold, I make all things new' (Rev. 21.5). Christians are introduced into this newness by baptism whereby they die to sin, 'so that as Christ was raised from the dead by the glory of the Father, we too might walk in *newness* of life' (Rom. 6.4). Moreover this newness is preserved and perpetuated by union with Christ in the eucharist. The common drinking of the cup of blessing is a sharing in Christ's saving death and its effects[35] and those effects comprise the partaking of the new life that is the life of Christ communicated to us. So Paul can say that 'Christ lives in me' (Gal. 2.20); we are 'alive to God in Christ Jesus' (Rom. 6.11), as through the eucharist we are progressively re-created to become the new man or new humanity (Eph. 4.24). Baptism into Christ is then the re-creation of humankind in the image of God; communion with Christ is the continuation of that creative process. Eucharist and creativity as newness are at one.

Moreover the celebration of the eucharist now reveals that the present can be the time of the creative meeting with the past, through the recalling of the Christ event, and with the future, as we anticipate the consummation. The eucharist indeed is a fore-taste of the age to come; it is, as I have argued, a partial enjoyment in advance of the messianic banquet – it is therefore essentially about 'newness' and by its very nature is intended to be a creative occasion. But rightly understood the creative newness of the eucharist does not concern the Christian community alone. The church is to serve the future of the world and it is in order to create that future that the liturgical assembly comes together. Hence in the words of C. Duchesneau,

> the liturgy should not cease revealing at the present time the future of the world of which the church is the sign. The liturgy should not cease creating, in the present of the church, the future of the world.[36]

The second aspect of creativity to which I have called attention above is freedom, i.e. creativity arises from and leads towards liberty. To speak of freedom in relation to worship is to place a serious question mark against forms of service that are entirely

inherited from the past and are so rigid in their requirements –
because of either a text handed down or the domination of an
ordained minister – that no freedom for creative response is possible.[37]* But the liturgy is not primarily a matter of texts and prescribed ceremonies, but of people called to be co-creators with the
Creator they are honouring. Worship begins with human beings
and not with books, not even with prayer books.

It follows from what has just been said that there must be opportunity for the members of a congregation to exercise their talents in
the course of worship. If there is no possibility of this, then three
adverse consequences will ensue: first, the grace-gifts that are intended to build up the congregation (I Cor. 14.5) will not fulfil the
purpose of their bestowal; second, the community will then suffer
because not to use one's gifts is to fail to make one's own contribution to the whole; third, the gifts are likely to atrophy because it
is only by exercising them that they can be developed.

For some the gifts will be of the aesthetic or artistic type, i.e. to
one is given the gift of painting or drawing, to another of playing
an instrument, to another of dancing, to another of singing. Many
people have considerable acting talents, while others are endowed
with humour and can tell amusing stories – they can help us to
laugh before the Lord. Paul was not producing an exhaustive but a
typical catalogue of gifts, referring both to daily life and worship,
when he said:

> Having gifts that differ according to the grace given to us, let us use
> them: if prophecy, in proportion to our faith; if service, in our serv-
> ing; he who teaches, in his teaching; he who exhorts, in his exhorta-
> tion; he who contributes, in liberality; he who gives aid, with zeal; he
> who does acts of mercy, with cheerfulness (Rom.12.6ff.).

Not to bring these gifts to God in worship is to deny their source
and to be guilty of ingratitude. Not to exercise them before God is
to become passive, but active participation in the eucharist – and
this was the burden of my preceding analysis – does not mean a
mere following in the mind, but expression in word, music and
gesture.[38] A congregation, as we have seen, is not the same as an
audience in a theatre; its impotence to effect in any way the outcome of the play should not characterize a group participating in
worship. Nor indeed is worship to be like a play in which most of
the actors are dissatisfied with their roles or, worse, are just extras

standing around with little or nothing to do. Similarly a service that does not encourage creativity by allowing for the free exercise of our gifts makes those present feel unnecessary, not participants but onlookers or hearers – an audience, uninvolved and therefore unlikely to be missed if they absent themselves. Here perhaps is where the ordained minister may find his true liturgical role by looking 'for the locked up creativity in others in order somehow to release it'.[39] Worship could then really be a creative occasion because our gifts are being employed in praise of their bestower.

The third element in creativity passed previously in brief review is that which relates it to the image of God in terms of the Genesis creation myth. Human beings, made in the divine image, are called to be creators like their Creator. This theme is not confined to the Old Testament; it is also present in the Pauline writings where Christ is said to be 'the image of the invisible God' (Col. 1.15). Thus for the image in which we were created to be renewed in us we have 'to be conformed to the image of his Son' (Rom. 8.29). But how is this process initiated and continued? It is a recurring subject in Christian thought that restoration to the image begins at baptism. So, to give a single example and not to weary the reader by piling one illustration upon another, according to Ambrose of Milan: 'we are sealed that the Holy Spirit may portray in us the likeness of the heavenly image.'[40] But complete conformation to the image depends upon a process of union by growth and this is effected in us by partaking of Christ's body and blood in the eucharist. In other words, as we feed upon the one who is the image of God, the stamp of that heavenly image is more deeply imprinted upon us.[41] The eucharist is instrumental in the process of our continual refashioning in that image. But since this image is to be understood in terms of creativity, there is evident a very close link between creativity and the eucharist.

It is of course possible to speak of this subject by means of a slightly different vocabulary. The restoration of the divine image is one way of describing what is often referred to as salvation or wholeness. If we relate the two concepts – salvation and conformity to the image – then we can appreciate how it is possible to interpret being saved as being caught up in a dynamic process that focusses upon creativity. 'Art makes man whole, and man is whole when he engages in art.'[42] Now the meaning of baptism and of the eucharist is often expounded in terms of salvation or wholeness.

Just as baptism is a sharing in the death of Christ (Rom. 6.3), so the eucharist is a present partaking of his passion.[43] Similarly because of the baptismal co-death with Christ there is conveyed remission of sins (Acts 22.16), so too communion enables us to share in the fruits of Christ's saving action, including renewed forgiveness.[44] These are so many ways of referring to salvation, therefore to wholeness and so to creativity. Hence my repeated plea that the eucharist should be a creative occasion in order to be a ritual and instrument of wholeness. It needs to be this to reveal and embody something of that newness which is part of what the Kingdom of God is all about; it needs to have newness about it 'to show by the use of contemporary cultural elements that salvation is a present event for those who celebrate its author.'[45]

Let no one suppose that I am deluding myself by believing that to follow the path of creativity and to encourage full participation is to pursue an easy road. The arts and creativity in any form 'are not safe for any institution which seeks to avoid change, for they can challenge people to think about their lives and to alter them'.[46] Indeed to find new forms of life, new ways of living, new patterns of worship – all this is to take risks, which are no more, though no less, than, the necessary risks of creativity. Yet it is to this that Christ summons us and not to security, to dull routine, to repetitive prayers, to worship by rote.

REFERENCES

In the main these notes provide the sources of quotations and also references to related works, and these are all listed in the bibliography by section and number. The few that add something to the substance of passages in the book have been marked in the text with an asterisk (*).

Preface

1. J. W. Getzels and P. W. Jackson in Vernon (II.10), 201. I am not suggesting that there is no more to creativity than this, i.e. the subject is much more complex than just a contrast between convergence and divergence, cf. the remarks by L. Hudson, ibid., 227f.
2. Koestler (II.4)

1 *Play and Worship*

1. Guardini (VI.2)
2. Huizinga (VI.3)
3. Rahner (VI.6)
4. Neale (VI.5)
5. For an account of the application of games theory to many disciplines see Miller (VI.4)
6. For a criticism of the Protestant Ethic see Davies (IX.11), 194–213
7. Caillois (VI.1), 52
8. Rahner (VI.6), 35
9. Huizinga (VI.3), passim
10. Caillois (VI.1), 23f.
11. Neale (VI.5), 156
12. Guardini (VI.2), 104
13. Neale (VI.5), 21
14. Ibid., 23f.
15. Letter 15, para. 2, quoted by Rader and Jessup (II.6), 341f.
16. Letter 15, para. 9; ibid., 342
17. *Trad. Apost.*, x

18. Davies (IX.12)

19. Another example of the neglect of a Pauline rule was the continued use of Latin in the Roman Church long after it had ceased to be understood by the people, thus compromising the principle of intelligibility. Even those churches who adopted the vernacular long ago tend to perpetuate a specialized vocabulary and to use thought forms that mean little at the present day.

20. Caillois (VI.1), 52
21. Davies (IX.13)
22. Weber (V.12), 102
23. Neale (VI.5), 44
24. Ibid., 72
25. Davies (IX.11), 332f.
26. Neale (VI.5), 73
27. Cazeneuve (IX.5), 123
28. Davies (IX.11), 312–15
29. Debuyst (II.1), 5–9
30. Cox (IX.7), passim
31. Neale (VI.5), 56
32. Moltmann (VIII.26), 36
33. Caillois (VI.1), 27
34. Mol (V.10), 238
35. Neale (VI.5), 60
36. Ibid., 57
37. Ibid., loc. cit.
38. Davies (VIII.10), 85–92
39. Huizinga (VI.3), 14
40. Neale (VI.5), 82
41. Ibid., 84

2 *Dance and Worship*

1. Huizinga (VI.3)
2. Rahner (VI.6), 66
3. Huizinga (VI.3), 7
4. Ibid., passim
5. Rust (III.14), 3ff.
6. Huizinga (VI.3), 20
7. Ibid., 150
8. Valéry (III.18), 165ff.
9. Rust (III.14), 11
10. Valéry (III.17), 22ff.
11. Guardini (VI.2), 106
12. Cullmann and Leenhardt (IX.8), 46

13. Valéry (III.19), 149
14. Quoted by Klapp (v.7), 119
15. Armitage (III.2), 103
16. Ibid., 104
17. Garaudy (III.8), 13
18. Duncan (III.5), 94
19. Quoted by Garaudy (III.8), 87
20. Ibid., 139
21. Valéry (III.18), 175
22. Davies (III.3)
23. Van Peursen (VIII.30), 34–49
24. Cicero, *Pro Murena*. vi. 13
25. *Hom. 47 in Julian. Mart.*
26. *Hom. 23 de Novilum.*
27. Van Peursen (VIII.30), 18–33
28. Quoted by Garaudy (III.8), 77
29. It should be noted that when Paul speaks of 'flesh' in a derogatory manner, he is using the term not to denigrate our physical nature but to refer to our manner of life which is the occasion for sin, cf. Van Peursen (VIII.30), 95–103
30. *De Carne Christi*, 4
31. Duncan (III.5), 187
32. Harper (III.9), 221
33. Keen (III.10), 2
34. Lucian, *De Saltatione*, 6
35. Garaudy (III.8), 16
36. Rahner (VI.6), 6
37. Brunner (VIII.4), 502
38. Valéry (III.19), 146
39. Davies (IX.11), 67
40. Lowen (III.11), 2
41. It may be noted that promiscuity can also be a desperate, and vain, attempt to gain some contact with the body.
42. Lowen (III.11), 93
43. Ibid., 47
44. Oesterley (III.13), 80
45. Lowen (III.11), 298
46. McGill (III.12), 19
47. McCabe (VIII.22), 91
48. Garaudy (III.8), 69
49. Ibid., 78
50. Herzog (VIII.14), 36
51. Duncan (III.5), 200
52. Lowen (III.11), 140

53. Ibid., 258
54. vii. 1
55. Garaudy (III.8), 16
56. Eaton (III.6)
57. These theses are somewhat baldly stated; for a full discussion of the basis upon which they rest see Part II of Davies (IX.11)
58. Garaudy (III.8), 25
59. Duncan (V.4), 374
60. McGill (III.12), 182
61. Ibid., 184
62. Herzog (VIII.14), 75, 59
63. Davies (IX.11), 278
64. Ibid., 336
65. Quoted by Garaudy (III.8), 120
66. *Politics*, viii. 1340A
67. Quoted by Garaudy (III.8), 120
68. I have expanded this subject in the Epilogue
69. Garaudy (III.8), 20
70. Ibid., 128
71. Keen (III.10), 52
72. Oesterley (III.13), 154
73. *De Sacramentis*, 5.14
74. *Comm. in Zach.* 2.8. The quotation from II Kingdoms (II Sam.) 6.22 is from the LXX
75. Klapp (V.7), 190
76. Walker (III.20), 30
77. Garaudy (III.8), 196
78. Bocock (IX.2), 37, 163
79. This argument is strongly advanced by Foatelli (III.7)
80. Quoted by Andrews (III.1), 146
81. Singer (III.15), 114, 118
82. Keen (III.10), 159
83. Taylor (III.16)

3 Sexuality and Worship

1. Lampe (V.9)
2. Berdyaev (VIII.2), 295
3. Solovyev (VIII.29)
4. Williams (VIII.31)
5. Doms (VIII.11)
6. Davies (VIII.7), 211–20; (IX.11), 158–72
7. In what follows I have adopted the admirable exegesis of Bonnard (V.2), 65f.

8. Lewis (VIII.19), 109
9. Davis (III.4), 41
10. Ibid., loc. cit.
11. Ibid., 140
12. Ibid., 133
13. Lewis (VIII.18), 27
14. Quoted by Garaudy (III.8), 177
15. Quoted by Rogers (I.10), 63
16. Ibid., 62
17. Quoted ibid. 64
18. *Ad Uxorem*, II.4
19. 8.11
20. Davies (III.4), 42
21. Böckle (VIII.3)
22. Cf. Bocock (IX.2), 147

4 *Conflict and Worship*

1. *Apol.* 1.65
2. *De Orat.* 18
3. *Didache*, xiv.1f.
4. *Didascalia*, ii.45
5. Dix (IX.16), 106
6. *Didascalia*, ii.54
7. *Const. Ap.*, 2.54
8. Brightman (IX.3), 382
9. Ibid., 434
10. Ibid., 462
11. Jungmann (IX.21), 48
12. Davies (I.3), 186f.
13. In Mathews (I.7), 329
14. Macquarrie (I.6), 32
15. Coser (I.1), 85
16. Houtart and Rémy (v.6), 270
17. Freire (I.4), 32
18. *The Marriage of Heaven and Hell*, 3, 9
19. Simmel (I.11), 15
20. Coser (I.1), 154
21. Ibid., 126f.
22. Simmel (I.11), 13f.
23. Coser (I.1), 157
24. Houtart and Rémy (v.6), 273
25. Crow (I.2), 303ff.
26. Wattenberg (I.13), 154–61

27. Robers (1.10), 28
28. Ibid., 34
29. Williams (1.14), passim
30. Davies (VIII.9), 62
31. *English Hymnal*, 135
32. Ibid., 145
33. Eaton (III.6), 8f.
34. Segundo (VIII.28), 44
35. Assmann (VII.1), 139
36. Garcia and Calle (VIII.12), 72ff.
37. Davies (IX.11), 226f.; (1.3), 115
38. Richardson (VIII.27), 98-9
39. Lambourne (VIII.17), 90
40. Rogers (1.10), 11
41. In Lee and Marty (1.5), 177
42. Miller and Swanson (1.8), 74
43. Mol (V.10), 31
44. Ibid., 22
45. Klein (V.8), 121
46. *Sermo* 57.7
47. *In Joann. Hom.* 46; cf. Davies (VIII.7), 106-9, 131ff.
48. Oden (1.9), 38f.
49. H. M. Moore in Spregel (1.12), 339
50. Andrews (III.1), 151

5 Politics and Worship

1. So Schmidt (VII.10)
2. Cf. Cullinan (VII.4)
3. Assmann (VII.1), 34f.
4. Davies (1.3), 11ff.
5. Wilson (IX.28), 241
6. Machoveč (VIII.21), 88
7. Ibid., 19
8. Davies (1.3), 28f.
9. de Clerq (IX.14), 128
10. Howe (VIII.15), 84
11. Gelineau (IX.20), 156
12. Miranda (VIII.25), 57
13. Ibid., 59
14. Guichard (VII.7), 55ff.
15. Garcia and Calle (VIII.12), 72f.
16. Davies (1.3), 115
17. Cone (VIII.6), 12

18. Metz (VIII.23), 21–4
19. Cone (VIII.6), 126
20. Schmidt (VII.10), 21
21. Galilea (IX.18), 334
22. Llopis (IX.22), 67
23. Bangkok (VIII.1), 89
24. Cone (VIII.6), 125
25. Gelineau (IX.19), 109f.
26. Schillebeeckx (VII.9), 59
27. Cox (IX.7), 82f.
28. Moltmann (IX.23), 77
29. Duquoc (VII.5), 128
30. Segundo (VIII.28), 40
31. Miguez-Bonino (VIII.24), 64
32. Segundo (IX.26), 59
33. Duquoc (VII.5), 120
34. Meyer (IX.24), 49
35. Cone (VIII.6), 202
36. de Clerq (IX.15), 115
37. Machoveč (VIII.21), 85
38. Soelle (VII.12), 5f.
39. Moltmann (IX.23), 75
40. Ibid., 80
41. Gelineau (IX.19), 115
42. Petulla (VII.8), 174
43. Segundo (IX.26), 4
44. Davies (IX.13), 7–12
45. Soelle (VII.12), 89
46. *In Search* (VII.11), 144
47. Barth (VII.2), 74
48. Quoted by Coste (VII.3), 121
49. I am reproducing a point I made originally in Davies (IX.10), 100
50. G. Gutiérrez in his introduction to Assmann (VII.1), 8
51. Howe (II.3), 223
52. Davies (VIII.8)
53. Gollwitzer (VII.6), 5
54. Davies (IX.11), 280, 331ff., 343f.

6 *Laughter and Worship*

1. Niebuhr in Hyers (IV.6), 149
2. Brown and Casalis (IV.2), 3
3. Freud (IV.4)
4. Bergson (IV.1)
5. Koestler (II.4), 51

6. Ibid., 77
7. For arguments in support of these theses see Davies (IX.11), 307
8. Ibid., 60ff.
9. This argument is presented at length in Davies (VIII.10)
10. Bultmann (VIII.5), 63
11. Hüsch (IV.5), 9
12. Ralph Moore as quoted by Howard Moody in Bloy (IX.1), 95
13. N. A. Scott in Hyers (IV.6), 50
14. Hyers (IV.6), 209
15. W. M. Zucker, ibid., 87
16. P. L. Berger, ibid., 126
17. Ibid., 139
18. Moore in Bloy (IX.1), 95
19. Berger in Hyers (IV.6), 127
20. Ibid., 130
21. For a brief account of the Feast of Fools see Davies (VIII.10), 53f., 81f.
22. Hyers (IV.6), 239
23. Ibid., 212
24. Coser (IV.3), 172
25. Santayana (IV.7), 138
26. For the rationale of creative liturgy see the first chapter of this book and Davies (IX.11), 307–51. Some account of forms of worship devised by the participants may be found in Cooke (IX.6), Elliott (IX.17) and Sequeira (IX.27)
27. Chad Walsh in Hyers (IV.6), 243

Epilogue: Participation and Creativity

1. Davies (IX.11), 291f.
2. 1 *Apol.* 65
3. Klapp (V.7), 318
4. Wright (V.13), 43ff., 81
5. Altick (V.1), 16
6. Ibid., 18
7. Procter and Frere (IX.25), 55
8. Cuming (IX.9), 68
9. Bishop Hobson (V.5), 171
10. Overall (V.11), 153
11. Cox (V.3), 112
12. Dix (IX.16), 624
13. Ibid., 671
14. Sayers (II.8), 37
15. Berdyaev (VIII.2), 183

16. So creative writing is always fresh, cf. the frequency with which we are ready to see a new production of a Shakespeare play
17. T. J. Shapiro in Vernon (II.10), 281
18. Spender (II.9), 306
19. Rader and Jessup (II.6), 23
20. Berdyaev (VIII.2), 163
21. Ibid., 189
22. Vernon (II.10), 140
23. Berdyaev (VIII.2), 169
24. To Butts, 10 January 1802
25. Laocoon
26. *Jerusalem* 77
27. Laocoon
28. To Hayley, 11 December 1805
29. Berdyaev (VIII.2), 169
30. Vernon (II.10), 139
31. Ibid., 356
32. Howe (II.3), 60
33. Sayers (II.7), 155
34. Lindsay (VIII.20), 50; cf. Nardone (II.5)
35. Kummel (VIII.16), 221
36. Duchesneau (II.2), 83
37. Davies (IX.13). However on occasion one may use experimental liturgies as an aid to the discovery of new possibilities, e.g. Brown and Yorke (IX.4)
38. Hebblethwaite (VIII.13), 29
39. Howe (II.3), 58
40. *De Spiritu Sancto* 1.79
41. Davies (VIII.7), 133–50
42. Rader and Jessup (II.6), 217
43. Davies (VIII.7), 127
44. Ibid., 128f.
45. Duchesneau (II.2), 73
46. Bocock (IX.2), 167f.

BIBLIOGRAPHY

For ease of reference this bibliography has been divided into sections, but of course some books could have been included under more than one heading. Unless otherwise stated, the place of publication is London.

In addition to this list of works consulted, I would also mention five articles of mine previously published by the Institute for the Study of Worship and Religious Architecture (ISWRA) in the University of Birmingham. These articles, incorporated in chapters 2, 3, 6 and in the Epilogue, have been rewritten, expanded and had new material added. They are as follows:

'Towards a Theology of the Dance', *Worship and Dance*, 1975, 43–56
'Eroticism, Dance and Christian Worship', ibid., 57–63
'Worship and Humour', *Research Bulletin*, 1975, 3–9
'Participation in Worship. Its Meaning and its Relation to Literacy' ibid., 1977, 3–10
'The Church and the Arts', *The Cathedral and the Arts*, 1976, 5–9

1 Conflict

1. L. A. Coser, *The Functions of Social Conflict*, Routledge and Kegan Paul, 1956
2. L. D. and A. Crow, *Adolescent Development and Adjustment*, MacGraw-Hill Book Co., New York, 1956
3. J. G. Davies, *Christians, Politics and Violent Revolution*, SCM Press and Orbis Books, New York, 1976
4. P. Freire, *Pedagogy of the Oppressed*, Herder and Herder, New York, 1970, Penguin Books 1972
5. R. Lee and M. Marty (eds), *Religion and Social Conflict*, Oxford University Press, New York, 1962
6. J. Macquarrie, *The Concept of Peace*, SCM Press 1973
7. Z. K. Mathews (ed.), *Responsible Government in a Revolutionary Age*, SCM Press 1966
8. D. R. Miller and G. E. Swanson, *Inner Conflict and Defence*, Holt, New York, 1960

9. T. C. Oden, *The Intensive Group Experience. The New Pietism*, Westminster Press, Philadelphia, 1972

10. C. R. Rogers, *Encounter Groups*, Allen Lane 1971

11. G. Simmel, *Conflict and the Web of Group-Affiliations*, Free Press, Glencoe, Illinois, 1955

12. H. B. C. Spregel (ed.), *Citizen Participation in Urban Development*, 2, NTL Institute for Applied Behavioral Science, Washington, 1969

13. W. W. Wattenberg, *The Adolescent Years*, Harcourt-Brace, New York, 1955

14. H. A. Williams, *Tensions, Necessary Conflicts in Life and Love*, Mitchell Beazley 1976

II *Creativity*

1. F. Debyust, *Architecture and Christian Celebration*, Lutterworth Press and John Knox Press, Richmond, Virginia, 1968

2. C. Duchesneau, 'Improvisations sur le thème de la créativité liturgique', *Maison-Dieu*, 111, 1972, 70–83

3. R. L. Howe, *The Creative Years*, Seabury Press, New York, 1969

4. A. Koestler, *The Act of Creation*, Hutchinson 1964

5. H. F. Nardone, 'Creativity in Art and Ethics', *Journal of Aesthetic and Art Criticism*, 34, 1975, 183–90

6. M. Rader and B. Jessup, *Art and Human Values*, Prentice-Hall, Englewood Cliffs, 1976

7. D. L. Sayers, *The Mind of the Maker*, Methuen 1941

8. — *Unpopular Opinions*, Gollancz 1946

9. S. Spender, *World within World*, Hamish Hamilton 1951

10. P. E. Vernon, *Creativity*, *Selected Readings*, Penguin Books, Harmondsworth, 1973

III *Dance*

1. E. D. Andrews, *The Gift to be Simple. Songs, Dance and Rituals of the American Shakers*, Dover Publications, New York, 1967

2. M. Armitage, *Martha Graham*, Dance Horizons Inc., New York, 1966

3. J. G. Davis, 'Dancing in Church Buildings', *Worship and Dance*, ISWRA, Birmingham, 1975, 16–21

4. C. Davies, *Body as Spirit. The Nature of Religious Feeling*, Hodder and Stoughton 1976

5. Isadora Duncan, *My Life*, Gollancz 1968

6. J. H. Eaton, 'Dancing in the Old Testament', *Worship and Dance*, ISWRA, Birmingham, 1975, 4–15

7. R. Foatelli, *Les danses religieuses dans le christianisme*, Editions Spes, Paris, 1938

8. R. Garaudy, *Danser sa vie*, Editions du Seuil, Paris, 1973

9. P. Harper, 'Discussion on Dance', *Theoria to Theory*, 8, 1974

10. S. Keen, *To a Dancing God*, Harper and Row, New York, 1970

11. A. Lowen, *The Betrayal of the Body*, Macmillan, New York, 1967

12. A. C. McGill, *The Celebration of the Flesh*, *Poetry in Christian Life*, Association Press, New York, 1964

13. W. O. E. Oesterley, *The Sacred Dance*, Oxford University Press 1923

14. F. D. Rust, *Dance in Society*, Routledge and Kegan Paul 1969

15. I. Singer, *Santayana's Aesthetics*, Greenwood Press, Westport, Connecticut, 1973

16. M. F. Taylor, *A Time to Dance. Symbolic Movement in Worship*, United Church Press, Philadelphia, Boston, 1967

17. P. Valéry, *Degas Danse Dessin*, Gallimard, Paris, 14th ed., 1938

18. —*Philosophie de la danse* (1936) in *Oeuvres*, 11, Editions de la N.R.F., Paris, 1939

19. —*Eupalinos and L'âme et la danse*, ed. V. J. Daniel, Oxford University Press 1967

20. J. L. Walker, *Body and Soul. Gestalt Therapy and Religious Experience*, Abingdon Press, Nashville, 1971

IV *Laughter*

1. H. Bergson, *Laughter. An Essay on the Meaning of the Comic*, Macmillan 1911

2. R. McAfee Brown and G. Casalis, *Portrait of Karl Barth*, Doubleday, New York, 1963

3. R. L. Coser, 'Some Social Functions of Laughter. A Study of Humour in a Hospital Setting', *Human Relations*, 12, 1959, 171–82

4. S. Freud, *Jokes and their Relation to the Unconscious*, Routledge and Kegan Paul 1960

5. H. D. Hüsch, 'I'd Like to be a Clown', *Salvation Today and Contemporary Experience. A Collection of Texts for Critical Study and Reflection*, WCC, Geneva, 1972 (originally published in 'Archeblues und andere Sprechgesänge', Sanssouci Verlag, Zürich)

6. M. Conrad Hyers (ed.), *Holy Laughter. Essays on Religion in the Comic Perspective*, Seabury Press, New York, 1969

7. G. Santayana, *Soliloquies in England and Later Soliloquies*, Scribner, New York, 1922

V *Miscellaneous*

1. R. D. Altick, *The English Common Reader*, University of Chicago, Chicago, 1957

2. P. Bonnard, *L'évangile selon Saint Matthieu*, Delachaux et Niestlé, Neuchâtel and Paris, 1967

3. J. C. Cox, *Churchwardens' Accounts*, The Antiquary's Books 1913

4. H. D. Duncan, *Communication and Social Order*, Oxford University Press 1968

5. Bishop Hobson (ed.), *Church-Wardens' Accounts*, Somerset Record Society, 4, 1890

6. F. Houtart and J. Rémy, *Eglise et société en mutation*, Mame, Tour, 1969

7. O. E. Klapp, *Collective Search for Identity*, Holt, Rinehart and Winston, New York, 1969

8. J. Klein, *Working in Groups*, Hutchinson 1963

9. G. W. H. Lampe, *A Patristic Greek Lexicon*, Clarendon Press, Oxford, 1961

10. H. Mol, *Identity and the Sacred*, Blackwell, Oxford, 1976

11. W. H. Overall, *The Accounts of the Churchwardens of the Parish of St Michael, Cornhill, in the City of London from 1456 to 1608*, n.d.

12. M. Weber, *The Sociology of Religion*, Beacon Press, Boston, 1964

13. L. B. Wright, *Middle-Class Culture in Elizabethan England*, Oxford University Press 1935

VI *Play*

1. R. Caillois, *Les jeux et les hommes*, Gallimard, Paris, 1958

2. R. Guardini, *The Spirit of the Liturgy*, Sheed and Ward 1930

3. J. Huizinga, *Homo Ludens. A Study of the Play-Element in Culture*, Routledge and Kegan Paul 1949

4. D. L. Miller, *Gods and Games. Towards a Theology of Play*, World Publishing Company, New York, 1969

5. R. E. Neale, *In Praise of Play. Towards a Psychology of Religion*, Harper and Row, New York, 1969

6. H. Rahner, *Man at Play*, Burns and Oates 1965

VII *Politics (and Political Theology)*

1. H. Assmann, *Practical Theology of Liberation*, Search Press 1975

2. K. Barth, *The Church and the Political Problems of Our Day*, Hodder and Stoughton, 1939

3. R. Coste, *Evangile et politique*, Aubier-Montaigne, Paris, 1968

4. T. Cullinan, *Eucharist and Politics* (Justice Paper No. 2), Catholic Institute for International Relations, n.d.

5. C. Duquoc, J. Guichard *et al.*, *Politique et vocabulaire liturgique*, Editions du Cerf, Paris, 1975

6. H. Gollwitzer, *The Rich Christians and Poor Lazarus*, St Andrews Press, Edinburgh, 1970

7. J. Guichard, *Eglise, luttes des classes et stratégies politiques*, Editions du Cerf, Paris, 1972

8. J. Petulla, *Christian Political Theology. A Marxian Guide*, Orbis Books, New York, 1972

9. E. Schillebeeckx, 'Critical Theories and Christian Political Commitment', *Concilium*, 4.9, 1973, 48–61

10. H. Schmidt, 'Lines of Political Action', *Concilium*, 2.10, 1974, 13–33

11. *In Search of a Theology of Development. A Sodepax Report*, 1970

12. D. Soelle, *Political Theology*, Fortress Press, Philadelphia, 1974

VIII *Theology*

1. *Bangkok 1973*, WCC Geneva, 1973

2. N. Berdyaev, *The Destiny of Man*, Bles 1937

3. F. Böckle, 'The Church and Sexuality', *Concilium*, 9.10, 1974, 144–55

4. E. Brunner, *The Divine Imperative*, Lutterworth Press, 2nd imp., 1942

5. R. Bultmann, *Existence and Faith*, Fontana 1946

6. J. H. Cone, *God of the Oppressed*, Seabury Press, New York, 1975

7. J. G. Davies, *The Spirit, the Church and the Sacraments*, Faith Press 1954

8. —*Members One of Another. Aspects of Koinonia*, Mowbray 1958

9. —*He Ascended into Heaven. A Study in the History of Doctrine*, Lutterworth Press and Association Press, New York, 1958

10. —*The Secular Use of Church Buildings*, SCM Press and Seabury Press, New York, 1968

11. H. Doms, *The Meaning of Marriage*, Sheed and Ward 1939

12. J. A. Garcia and C. R. Calle (eds), *Camilo Torres, Priest and Revolutionary*, Sheed and Ward 1968

13. P. Hebblethwaite, *The Runaway Church*, Collins 1975

14. H. Herzog, *Liberation Theology*, Seabury Press, New York, 1972

15. R. L. Howe, *Man's Need and God's Action*, Seabury Press, New York, 1966

16. W. G. Kümmel, *The Theology of the New Testament*, SCM Press, and Abingdon, 1974

17. R. A. Lambourne, *Community, Church and Healing*, Darton, Longman and Todd 1967

18. C. S. Lewis, *Christian Behaviour*, Bles 1943

19. — *The Four Loves*, Bles 1960, Fontana edition 1963

20. A. D. Lindsay, *The Two Moralities*, Eyre and Spottiswoode 1940

21. M. Machoveč, *A Marxist Looks at Jesus*, Darton, Longman and Todd 1976

22. H. McCabe, *Law, Love and Language*, Sheed and Ward 1968
23. J. B. Metz, 'The Future in the Memory of Suffering', *Concilium*, 6.8, 1972, 9–25
24. J. Miguez-Bonino, *Doing Theology in a Revolutionary Situation*, Fortress Press, Philadelphia, 1975
25. J. P. Miranda, *Marx and the Bible. A Critique of the Philosophy of Oppression*, Orbis Books, New York, 1974, SCM Press 1977
26. J. Moltmann, *Theology and Joy*, SCM Press and Harper and Row, New York, 1973
27. A. Richardson, *The Miracle-Stories of the Gospels*, SCM Press 1942
28. J. L. Segundo, *The Liberation of Theology*, Orbis Books, New York, 1976, Gill and Macmillan 1977
29. V. Solovyev, *The Meaning of Love*, Bles 1945
30. C. A. Van Peursen, *Body, Soul, Spirit: A Survey of the Body-Mind Problem*, Oxford University Press 1966
31. Charles Williams, *Religion and Love in Dante*, Dacre 1941

ix *Worship*

1. M. B. Bloy (ed.), *Multi-media Worship. A Model and Nine Viewpoints*, Seabury Press, New York, 1969
2. R. Bocock, *Ritual in an Industrial Society*, Allen and Unwin 1974
3. F. E. Brightman, *Liturgies Eastern and Western*, 1, Clarendon Press, Oxford, 1896
4. J. P. Brown and R. L. Yorke, *The Covenant of Peace. A Liberation Prayer Book by the Free Church of Berkeley*, Morehouse-Barker, New York, 1971
5. J. Cazeneuve, *Les rites et la condition humaine*, Presses universitaires, Paris, 1958
6. J. A. Cooke, 'Worship and the Underground Church', *Research Bulletin*, ISWRA, Birmingham, 1972, 7–15
7. H. Cox, *The Feast of Fools. A Theological Essay in Festivity and Fantasy*, Harvard University Press 1969
8. O. Cullmann and F. J. Leenhardt, *Essays on the Lord's Supper*, Lutterworth Press and John Knox Press, Richmond, Virginia, 1958
9. G. J. Cuming, *A History of the Anglican Liturgy*, Macmillan 1969
10. J. G. Davies, *Worship and Mission*, SCM Press and Association Press, New York, 1967
11. — *Every Day God. Encountering the Holy in World and Worship*, SCM Press, 1973
12. — 'The Influence of Architecture upon Liturgical Change', *Studia Liturgica*, 9.4, 1973, 231–40
13. — 'The Limitations of Liturgical Revision', *Looking to the Future*.

Prospects for Worship, Religious Architecture and Socio-Religious Studies,
ed., J. G. Davies, ISWRA, Birmingham, 1976, 7–12

14. B. de Clerq, *Religion, idéologie et politique*, Casterman, Tournai,
1968

15. — 'Political Commitment and Liturgical Celebration', *Concilium*,
4.9, 1973, 110–16

16. G. Dix, *The Shape of the Liturgy*, Dacre, 1945

17. E. Elliott, 'Local Creative Liturgy', *Research Bulletin*, ISWRA,
Birmingham 1973, 7–27

18. S. Galilea, 'Les messes de protestation', *Parole et messe*, 14, 1971

19. J. Gelineau, 'Celebrating the Paschal Liberation', *Concilium*, 2.10,
1974, 107–19

20. — *Demain la liturgie, Essai sur l'évolution des assemblées chrétiennes*,
Editions du Cerf, Paris, 1976

21. J. A. Jungmann, *The Mass of the Roman Rite*, Benzinger Bros,
New York, 1959

22. J. Llopis, 'The Message of Liberation in the Liturgy', *Concilium*,
2.10, 1974, 65–77

23. J. Moltmann, 'The Liberating Feast', *Concilium*, 2.10, 1974, 74–84

24. H. B. Meyer, 'The Social Significance of the Liturgy', *Concilium*,
2.10, 1974, 34–50

25. F. Procter and W. H. Frere, *A History of the Book of Common
Prayer*, Macmillan, 1941

26. J. L. Segundo, *The Sacraments Today* (*A Theology for Artisans
of a New Humanity*, 4), Orbis Books, New York, 1974

27. A. R. Sequiera, 'Creative Liturgy: A Practical Model', *Worship
and Dance*, ISWRA, Birmingham, 1975, 64–75

28. M. Wilson, 'Nyakyusa Ritual and Symbols', *American Anthropologist*, 56, 1954, 228–41

INDEX